DIVINE DYNAMITE

DIVINE DYNAMITE

Entering
Awakening's Heartland

ROBERT AUGUSTUS MASTERS

Tehmenos Press

Note for Librarians: a cataloguing record for this
book that includes Dewey Decimal Classification and
US Library of Congress numbers is available from
the Library and Archives of Canada. The complete
cataloguing record can be obtained from their online
database at:
www.collectionscanada.ca/amicus/index-e.html
ISBN 1-4120-3633-X
Printed in Victoria, BC, Canada

Tehmenos Press

in association with:

TRAFFORD

Offices in Canada, USA, Ireland, UK and Spain
This book was published *on-demand* in cooperation
with Trafford Publishing. On-demand publishing
is a unique process and service of making a book
available for retail sale to the public taking advantage
of on-demand manufacturing and Internet marketing.
On-demand publishing includes promotions, retail
sales, manufacturing, order fulfilment, accounting and
collecting royalties on behalf of the author.
Book sales for North America and international:
Trafford Publishing, 6E–2333 Government St.,
Victoria, BC v8t 4p4 CANADA
phone 250 383 6864 (toll-free 1 888 232 4444)
fax 250 383 6804; email to orders@trafford.com
Book sales in Europe:
Trafford Publishing (UK) Ltd., Enterprise House,
Wistaston Road Business Centre, Wistaston Road,
Crewe, Cheshire cw2 7rp UNITED KINGDOM
phone 01270 251 396 (local rate 0845 230 9601)
facsimile 01270 254 983; orders.uk@trafford.com
Order online at:
www.trafford.com/robots/04-1461.html

10 9 8 7 6 5 4 3 2

TABLE of CONTENTS

Introduction:
Entering Awakening's Heartland

So solid this does seem
So firmly framed and named
Too real to be a dream
So it does appear
Until once again unraveled
Losing shape and gaining depth
Eyes behind my eyes opening
Without a thought

Naked and bleeding I crawl
From all the debris
That just a breath or so ago
Called itself me

Let all the words sink
Sink like lead through oceans of cloud
Sink like bait for deep-sea wonders
Sink, sink out of sight
Until what they describe
Rises bright and freshly bare
Looking, looking through
Our undreaming eyes at itself
Seeing what is out of sight

Sailing semantic seas can so easily leave us adrift somewhere behind our forehead, riding plastic waves, dreaming that we are not dreaming, unless we let ourselves be transported across the gap between language and what language represents.

This, of course, asks much of us. Sometimes what we are reading invites us to thus leap, perhaps even accompanying us in our crossing, holding us without holding us back. Through the words and between the lines, we may at such times feel the kinship, the steps, the pulse and spirit of the author, whose differences from us only make more vividly compelling the similarities.

In our passage to the essential—our journey into what we never really left but only dreamt we did—we eventually begin to recognize ourselves in and through each other, intuiting our collective condition and opportunity, knowing ourselves to be more than we can imagine, grateful for, among other things, the word-boats that helped get us out on the open sea.

Each journey, however strange, is our journey. We are all, all dying to live. Each life, however short or mundane, uniquely and eloquently expresses this. Each note enriches the music. The music we make makes us. Everything passes, but the music goes on. Thus do we outlive ourselves.

All our possible pasts don't add up to us. In leaving their warp and weave, keeping only their necessary teachings, their essential kernel of reminder, we pass through Eternity's grinder, dying into the Real, finding freedom through becoming intimate with all that we are, and therefore with all that is.

Divine Dynamite is a community of writings held together by a stubborn passion for a deeper life, a life of full-blooded awaring and integration, a life in which everything—*everything*—is permitted to awaken us.

Much of *Divine Dynamite* is a turning toward what is typically turned away from. Its embrace of the One does not separate it from the Many. Its spirituality requires no distance from the raw, difficult, dirty, disreputable, or stuck. Hence it leans more toward intimacy than transcendence.

The Awakening process can be very fiery. In its flames what gets consumed, what dies, makes room for a deeper life. Until that fire is but light, we have work to do, work that these writings are devoted to exploring and honoring. Such work is the ultimate labor of love. It is what we were born to do. It is our gift to all.

Some of *Divine Dynamite's* writings sing, some bleed, some rant, some attempt to say what is probably better left unsaid, but all are invitations, however roughly wrapped, to more fully enter Awakening's heartland, whether done like an eagle riding a wave of everlasting morning, or, more likely, on our hands and knees.

Greetings to the you who has already arrived, and greetings to the you who is still arriving. Both are equally welcome. Have a seat; the table is set, the wine uncorked, the food and company ready.

Robert Augustus Masters
Crescent Beach, British Columbia, July 2004

CHAPTER 1

Such Raw Beauty

There is a heart-aching so sharp so sweet so bottomless that both shatters and reassembles us. Such terrible beauty accompanies it, such fathomless yearning, such exquisitely painful gratitude. Endless is this beauty. Upon its shores I break and spill, emptied of the familiarity that self-centers our days and ways.

So very soon we are gone, like dreams vanishing before morning's habits. Did we leave a mark? Only wingprints in endless sky, tracing evaporating goodbyes. Tombstones soon but stardust. Life is our signature, scrawled by the infinitely varied shape-takings of the Real. Such raw beauty, beauty to die for, beauty both to bow to and to be, beauty that simultaneously outlives and is us.

Death makes Life worth living. Death makes beauty unspeakably obvious. Death makes Love unsurpassably important. Death wakes us up. What better ally could we have than Death? Death gives all the same opportunity. Death leaves no one out.

Life is, among other things, a Near-Death Experience. The passing of all things breaks our heart open to what matters most of all. Only through intimacy with Death do we find intimacy with the Deathless.

Gazing into soft blue sky, dissolving in its boundless embrace, cradling each of its clouds, whether weeping or thundering or dancing. Beauty beyond beauty coupling with undisturbable peace, through their succulent embrace revealing—not explaining, but revealing—that each moment contains all moments. This the deep lovers cannot help but recognize, as they die into Joy, surrendering their all to the Beloved until they are but clearings for that One. Naked openness, owned by none and belonging to all.

Avoiding Death kills us. Are we not, when we truly tire of doing time and redecorating our cells, dying to live? Dying to really live, to fully live? Dying to stop pretending we are not pretending? Dying to at last enter and fully, fully embody the Life we were born to live? Such dying is but birth, a labor of love, a making room for a deeper Life. The tenderest upstart green cracks and splits open the concrete sea upon which we are shipwrecked. The messy Ecstasy of birth unravels our straitjacketed identity. We bleed and soar, waves breaking on ever-virgin shore, dying into the Undying.

Silence is our witness. Silence has seen it all. Silence cradles our pain until its ache wakes us.

Death doesn't happen to Life. Death serves Life. The beauty of it all, the hyperbole-transcending majesty and wonder of it all, both brings us to our knees and wings us. We go from survival to living, and from living to being lived, and from being lived to Being, losing everything along the way except what most matters. Loss breaks open the heart, dissolving its armoring. Loss gives beauty its true depth. Death is the mother of loss.

The blue fire of the dying poet's eyes makes ruggedly transparent art of his ravaged face. He cries out, his hoarsely impassioned words the last sigh of a vagabond wave, seafoam dying on some midnight beach. His freedom is in having no choice. His love empties his mind and leaves his body see-through. His final poem is an infinitely sadhappy smile as he freefalls into Death.

And what is his message for us? Let go, let your heart break, let your life be beauty made visible, let all things awaken you, let your life be Poetry, the music of Truth, the epiphanously idiosyncratic soulsong of significance. And all the words die so, so soon in an avalanche of Silence, their sound and meaning and audience gone. But how they danced in their bright sliver of a moment! And how we danced and loved and wept and blazed in our brief time!

The door is, as always, already open. Openness awaiting openness. The invitation that will not go away. We are dying to live. Let us not wait any longer. Let us do what it takes. There are not higher stakes.

CHAPTER 2

Divine Dynamite:
A Caveat
Regarding Spiritual Opening

When the night pulled back the bedcovers
And I sat knees-up ashaking
Seeking a sign sublime
My mind looking for the time
My body athrob with an Eternal rhyme
The windows, the windows did bulge with something unborn
Something I couldn't name
Something I could not contain

It is understatement in the extreme to say that spiritual opening is not necessarily a benign, nice, or comfortable process.

Initially we may flirt with spiritual opening, doing some meditation practices, reading spiritual or metaphysical literature, trying out different teachers and teachings, perhaps hoping that our spiritual experiences will make us happier or more successful, but when we go, or are compelled to go, beyond spiritual dilettantism and cultism, reaching the point where we don't give a damn about being spiritually correct, and where spiritual opening is not an option but a fundamental need, we find that it is more of a sacrificial process than we bargained for, necessarily bringing us face to face with all that we have turned away from, risen above, or otherwise avoided in ourselves.

O When the night pulled back the bedcovers
And my breath was not mine
And I knew, knew the Holy Design
And the Dark stormed my room so strangely bright
And my spine was a stem so green and so, so white

I did, I did give the night my hand
And let it lead me through a wild of shadowland

The self that is gung-ho about getting spiritual, that seeks transformation, that makes spiritual real estate out of moments of light, that defines itself through meditative practice and association with spiritual heavyweights, becomes, sooner or later, not only an object of awareness, but also fuel for the fire of Awakening—as eventually do *all* our selves, all the "I's" that together *make us up*.

This does not necessarily mean obliteration of our "I's", but rather enough of a ceasing to identify with them that there is little or no "I"—or convincingly separate self-sense—left to congratulate itself on having arrived spiritually. Spiritual awakening may seem like a very desirable bauble, a badge, a shining credential, for our egoity, but is actually its ultimate nightmare, its final bummer.

The fantasy "I" has about attending its own funeral is just narcissism stoned on spiritual greed. But there are no Oscars for awakening; there is no drama starring enlightened egoity or other impossibilities. Instead, there is freedom, freedom from self-obsessed subjectivity, freedom from identifying with anything in particular, freedom from dreaming that we are not dreaming, freedom to be.

O When the night pulled back the bedcovers
And I arose from the ruins of my dreams
And inside and outside were lovers
And exhale was inhale
And I glimpsed a love that could not fail
A love that was both ocean and sail
I did cry out for having so much and for wanting more
And for having done all this before

We may like the idea of waking up from all our dreaming, but when we begin to realize how much we have invested in our dreams, the possibility of waking up from them may lose much of its appeal. This, plus the fact that real spiritual practice cannot help but bring up everything that we'd rather keep down or shut away, is why so few pursue the farther reaches of spirituality. A comfortable, well-furnished stay in prison may seem preferable to the discomfort, the stretching, the out-on-the-edge times, that are as much a part of mature spiritual practice as are joy and equanimity.

So being in the crucible of Awakening's alchemy is not necessarily comfortable—the fire gives light, yes, but it also burns, generating enough heat to vaporize our illusions, lies, and trappings, if we will let ourselves get close enough to it.

Such fire destroys, but only in order to create. And heal. In its flames, our authenticity emerges, minus the case of mistaken identity with which we have burdened and obscured it.

Until the fire is but light, we will have to endure burning. Spiritual stamina. Whatever lies unresolved or unforgiven in us, whatever in us lies ostracized or condemned in some corner of our psyche, whatever in us has been kept in the dark—all will surface as we open spiritually. Initially this is bad news, but it is actually great news.

Sometimes working with the fire is easy, flowing, effortless, blissful, and sometimes it's hard work. There is no substitute for spending quality time in spiritual bootcamp. If we're ready, we don't have to sign up—circumstances set in motion by our actions and choices will enlist us, often seemingly against our will. If we really knew what we were getting into, not many of us would keep going in that direction. We may like to think we know what the optimal conditions are for our awakening, but the odds are that we don't know (and that we want it not to ask all that much of us). But Life "knows" and thus provides such conditions for us, for which we are, understandably, rarely grateful at the time.

> *And still I await the great night shining wild*
> *The great night so ripe with child*
> *An undreaming love inviting me to shed my fear*
> *Inviting me to give the night my hand*

Until I cannot help but look through the eyes
Of every face of every place

Spiritual openness may allow—or even invite—seemingly crazy or nonordinary phenomena to surface. If this gets out of control, as in what is termed a "spiritual emergency" (or in spirit-possession situations, as epitomized by Haitian and Balinese cathartic trances), it is not necessarily a problem, but may actually be an entirely fitting and profoundly healing process. Unfortunately, the more disruptive, disturbing, or painful difficulties associated with spiritual opening are often misconstrued as psychological disorders by health professionals.

Being out of control may actually be *needed* at a certain point, to break down unseen or unacknowledged repressive or dysfunctional structures that are not about to surface otherwise. Being out of control may propel one into the obviously spiritual, and also may shatter the subtle ossification that can occur when spirituality gets too "spiritual" for its own good. At the same time, however, it is important that one be able to—or be ably supported to—back off or put the brakes on when things get too crazy or scary.

Doing psychological work is very helpful both prior to and during spiritual opening. It's not enough to transcend one's "I's"—one must know, intimately know, one's psychological make-up, or its shadow elements will contaminate and skew one's spiritual efforts. Many have set sail with high hopes, only to get shipwrecked on the reefs of spiritual ambition. Premature immersion in the transpersonal guarantees reentry—more often than not on our hands and knees—into the personal, to at last get into what we were trying to avoid through our so-called spirituality. A foolproof process. No one gets through the Holy Gates who is not ready.

O Surrounded by fiery womb was I
The walls all aquiver
My mind no longer looking for the time
My body athrob with an Eternal rhyme

New growth running wild and velvet through my room
The windows, the windows a shattering of light
And my whole being did shiver and quake
Until my frame of mind did break
And I was in body what I was in spirit
The great night shining wild
The great night forever full of child

The nonconceptual realization of our actual condition is spiritual dynamite. Even a taste of it blows open doors we didn't even know existed.

And through those doors, through that clearing, is is-ness in the radical raw, beyond our wildest, craziest dreams, beyond even what "beyond" signifies. It's the ultimate Pandora's Box. So we play peekaboo with unmasked reality, cramming our glimpses of it in bottles destined to gather plenty of dust before they are uncorked. Too much light blinds. We thus tend to keep the bottles in the dark. Each glimpse—each satori—holds reality-unlocking potentials before which our humanness trembles and retreats. The only way to directly face God—God being That Which when realized liberates absolutely—is to lose face completely. When we face God we face far more than the far reaches of our humanness. We are more than we can imagine. We are not even a "we"…

And yet we are also this human being-ness, each of us uniquely personalized, as we reach for our meditation cushion or the remote control or the chunk of chocolate that we had in mind before beginning this essay. Beyond the nondual spiritual pabulum—we are all one, there is only God, etcetera, etcetera—currently being regurgitated for hungry ghosts satsanging with the latest spiritual biggies, and beyond the me-centered, semi-deified independence currently polluting contemporary culture, and beyond the conflict between spiritual approaches, are we, at once immeasurably vast and minute, at once deathless and dying, our universality and particularity inseparable, our shared heart having room for all.

We don't just have room for all; we *are* room for all, even as we simultaneously are the all for which we have room. Opening to this stops the mind in its tracks. Truth is what is intuited when ontological paradox makes unexplainable yet total sense. A poem struggles to tear its way out of its birthsac. It has so much to say that it says nothing. My train of thought is derailed. I don't mind. And my words, our words, the words, shatter, shatter like starlight upon rippling seas, so that the gap between them and what they describe narrows to nothing, leaving me speechless—at least for a few minutes—in the ever-fresh familiarity of Spirit, returned to what I never left but only dreamt I did.

CHAPTER 3

Everything
Serves Our Awakening

We are, as always, positioned to be Awakened by all things. The degree to which we recognize this is the degree to which we recognize that everything can be thus viewed and used. Everything, everyone, everywhere, everywhen. To not allow all things to further our Awakening keeps our relationship to—and appreciation of—Life partial, superficial, anemic, insufficiently intimate.

To be Awakened by all things is to be intimate with all things, including our resistance to such radical intimacy.

The key is in our hands but out of our grasp.

Our habits infiltrate, occupy, and surround us like monstrous children, their overfed appetites and spoilt automaticities squatting upon the throne of self. But they're just kids. Your kids, my kids, our kids. We let them keep us busy keeping up appearances.

Everything is all we've got, so we might as well stop expecting something else to do it for us. We need to stop making ourselves the pawn of salvation games. What's needed is not a new script or better role, but undreaming eyes.

It's all about attention. Attention usually is allowed to fasten to apparent objects, inner and outer. Something we see, hear, want, think about. Things to attend to, to get fasten-ated with. This may be deliberate, but much of the time it isn't. Observe how easily attention gets hooked to plans, judgments, fantasies, inner gossip, and other mental formations even when we desire otherwise. Attention as such—inattentive attention—makes its objects seem more real than they actually are. But attention can also be withdrawn, to varying degrees, from its objects. It can even be completely withdrawn, its sole focus being the very awareness of which it is but the focussing function.

The trick is, at least some of the time, to keep attention in-between its objects and its source. In so doing, Being becomes primary and perception secondary. Being-centered attention feels very different than ego-centered attention.

This is not about imposing a discipline on ourselves, but rather about yielding to a discipline that emerges primarily from Being. Along the way we have to traverse the warring territories occupied by the various "I's" that *make us up*. The ultimate dream journey. All that we meet, however alien, is us. Habits galore, addictions, longings, people and qualities and behaviors that catalyze every kind of emotion and reaction in us. So much hurt, grief, anger, shame, fear, numbness, and also so much joy and love, arising in the very same zones.

Let the painful assist you. Get more intimate with what hurts and bugs you. Date your loneliness, cuddle your grief, dance with your anger, cradle your shame. Stop making such a virtue out of comfort. Stop expecting spiritual practice to make you feel better. Get intimate with discomfort, without becoming masochistic or overly renunciatory. No flagellation is needed. There's no overseer screaming at the sperm to swim upstream. They may not know where they're going, but they're going there anyway, running all the red lights in eggistential ecstasy.

Everything can serve your Awakening, including the doubts or distractions with which you may now be flirting.

The perspective of Being offers a view unpolluted by any "I". Let it possess you. Allow it to mess and undress you, and look through your eyes. As this takeover empties you of your usual self, you'll discover that you're more you than ever before. Then you'll recognize yourself to be not just an "I"—or coalition of "I's"—but also *Being*, at once unbound and individuated. The perspective of Being does not stamp out differences, but rather clarifies them, even as it simultaneously renders them transparent to What-Really-Matters.

Being has no position. So long as we insist on maintaining a position, including that of having no position or of being "nobody", we will not significantly recognize Being.

Let your understanding of this be like a ripe fig still sun-warm and juicy and purple-plump, softly split open upon your appreciative palm, awaiting your lips and tongue and rising desire. This is not an understanding of the mind, but of the heart's depth, streaming through the body with a welcome too real to have meaning. So simple this is, lover-simple. It's the everfresh sublime Simplicity of the naked Real, effortlessly revealed through every shaping of Itself, every modification, every body.

If we look down upon the crippled or terminally solid in our flight, we will become unwinged, so that we might become more intimate with others' crutches and the dark side of our ascent.

Recognize—and remember to recognize—the Real in all that you see, hear, taste, smell, feel, and think, without reducing it to undifferentiated cosmic pabulum.

What we seek is forever unconcealed, hidden only by our insistence on having to have maps for it, paths, beliefs, rituals, spiritual ladders, as if it were actually out of reach. As always, what we seek is already here, inside our looking and outside every exterior, at once nowhere and everywhere, camouflaged by the apparitions of perception and self-deception.

Allow perception to become functionally secondary to Being.

The dragons guarding the treasure ask not to be slaughtered, but to be recognized. Through the gates we must go, leaving name and fame behind, passing through dark labyrinths, flayed open by the Minotaur's bleeding howl of recognition.

Do not pretend that you don't recognize or intuit that which would wean you from suckling the breasts of the familiar. Do not pretend that you don't know the Stranger at the Gate, your beloved's face in one hand, yours in the other, erased, ready again. And do not pretend that you are not pretending.

Homeward bound are they who, already brokenhearted, neither flee nor indulge in their pain, for in their woundedness, their lucid vulnerability, the Real *obviously* pulses. Homeward bound are they who, wronged or hurt, do not invest in righteousness or revenge, for in their openness, their willingness to fully forgive, they resonate with What-Really-Matters. Homeward bound are they who, ripened beyond conceit, are not trying to be anywhere other than where they are, for they not only are standing their true ground, but *are* it.

We don't even need to know what to do. It's more than enough to know what not to do, just so long as we don't make it into a program. The unmappable does not need cartography. Don't take this essay as instruction, regardless of my instructions. May my words, now staggering on fast fading legs, be of genuine benefit to you. May everything serve your awakening.

Everything.

CHAPTER 4

What Is Freedom?

F reedom, if it is real, is independent of circumstances. That is, it is not limited by its apparent limitations.

Freedom eludes and transcends all of its definitions (including those in this essay!). To say what it is is to create just one more word-house, one more container—however vastly conceived—from which freedom will eventually be sought.

Freedom is not a something we can possess, despite the commonplace languaging that suggests otherwise. Having the freedom to, for example, eat a certain food or pursue a particular career, simply implies the presence of a relatively unimpeded choice-making capacity—and such a capacity may itself actually be quite mechanical (and therefore *unchosen*). Calling this the freedom to be unfree may just distract us from the lack of real choice—and therefore the lack of freedom—in the very animation of "our" choice-making capacity.

But does this mean that freedom cannot exist without the capacity to consciously—that is, nonmechanically and nonreactively—make choices? Yes and no. Do animals have freedom? Are their choices really choices, or just conditioned preferences? We tend to view the tiger in the wild as being freer than the tiger in the zoo, even though both are still relating to their environments through their tiger-ness. The one in the wild has more options, but so too does the person in the usual life as compared to the person in a concentration camp.

So freedom is not about the number or even the quality of one's options. Our so-called choices can imprison us, further limit and burden us, bind and trap us, and our apparent lack of choice can liberate us, further open and release us, as when we allow unpleasant conditions to awaken us or render us more openhearted. Freedom thus does not mean liberation from limitation, but rather liberation *through* limitation.

Freedom is not about having a choice, but about not needing to have a choice. Freedom therefore does not depend upon conditions.

All of which is to say that Freedom is not in having, but in Being. Not being this, not being that, but *Being*.

We cannot *have* Freedom because at essence we *are* Freedom. Sartre famously said that we are doomed to Freedom—he's right insofar as there's no real or lasting escape from Freedom, but the negatively existential connotation with which he paints it says more about him than about Freedom itself. There are, of course, plenty of apparent escapes from Freedom, like slipping into an utterly mechanical life, but even then one could argue that such an escape from Freedom is itself a kind of freedom. The freedom to be unfree.

We are Freedom making an appearance.

There's no freedom from Freedom, at least not for very long. Sooner or later, the veils part, the blinders fall, and here we are once again, naked and nameless before the supreme openness of Freedom, feeling its indescribably familiar yet ever-fresh presence penetrating, embracing, and awakening us.

We can play peekaboo with Freedom for as long as we like, lost in our games of power and glory and love and obsession, but eventually we simply have to make a break for it, bursting toward what's most central of all, impassioned with the second innocence, the awakened innocence, of ripened humanity, crying out as we once did in our nothing-held-back childhood tag-adventures, "Home free!", until our adult-erated games lose their grip on us and fade, ultimately leaving us so free that we don't even conceive of ourselves as free.

Home free, Homed by Freedom. And all our history starts settling into what it has been all along, leaving us more at Home everywhere and everywhen, about which Silence, as always, has the last word.

CHAPTER 5

Turn Not from
Your Own Turning Away

Do not be so misled by endarkened feeling that you asylum it. If you keep shuttering its rooms, keep sealing it off, keep rejecting or otherwise disowning it, such feeling will become even more desperate and badly behaved, seeking your attention in whatever way it can, however destructive or painful.

But reach into that subterranean cell, that limping darkness, that emotional ghetto, that despair crowded with loneliness, and reach in wholeheartedly, and what is in there will eventually start reaching out to you all unfisted and vulnerably atremble, snugly fitting into your embrace, revealing itself to be not a problematic it, but rather reclaimed you.

There is no real escape from our hidden or orphaned or outcast selves. If we keep denying them the attention that they need, we remain crippled, partial, fragmented, overassociating ourselves with purity and cleanliness while we pollute ourselves with higher-than-thou moral pretensions.

Turn not from the beggar, so that you might cease degrading yourself. Turn not from the lame, so that you might cease hobbling yourself. Turn not from those who have turned away from you, so that you might better know the you who would reject or dehumanize others. Turn not from your own dark impulses, not so as to yield to their imperatives, but so as to meet them with such commanding tenderness that they serve rather than oppose your seedling Buddhahood. Turn not from your own turning away, so that you might enter a truer intimacy with your every shadow-self, rather than just homesteading in—and making the best of—a divided selfhood.

This is not the Pollyanesque slumming of the so-called Higher's mission to "help" or "enlighten" the so-called Lower. It is not charity. It is untainted by pity and spiritual ambition. It is not "got-it-together" us tossing a Christmas turkey to what we're keeping half-maddened in the cellar.

In a culture obsessed with status, it's no surprise that we gravitate toward adding more and more self-glamorizing experiences to our spiritual resumé—so as to presumably be sufficiently credentialed to get our ass through the Holy Gates. Such a passage will, however, remain but a fantasy or religious carrot for us so long as we define ourselves through what we possess or have accumulated, including our supposed identity. Only the naked can be clothed in God's Raiment.

Do not limit God to the Transcendental. To properly feast at the Holy Table, you need your appetite. To truly benefit from the Holy Light, you need to be at home with all your colors. To realize your inherent inseparability from God, you need to already be distinctly and substantially formed, having allowed the idiosyncratic crystallization of something convincingly separate, namely your self, that can be relieved of its illusory independence. Such dissolution or absorption, or, better, sublime integration, signals not the end of you, but rather the Truth of you, at once individuated and utterly undifferentiated. The drop is in the ocean, the ocean in the drop.

Truth is the heart of paradox, the revelatory logic of Being. It does not make sense to the rational mind because the rational mind cannot grasp it. Freedom begins when paradox is no longer paradoxical to us.

Do not make a problem out of the breaking of your heart, for such apparent tragedy is but the field ploughed deep and ready for the seeds of needed revelation and change.

The Sacred knocks at our door, having received little or no response when It simply stood before us. Heed not Its knocking, and a louder or more forceful—or more attention-grabbing—version of It will eventually pay us a visit, gatecrashing our slumber party. Thus do we invite in crises—the Sacred in clobbering drag. Heed not the lessons embedded in the crisis, and we'll likely become even more obsessed with protecting what we take ourselves to be—no one will be fully trusted by us, thereby leaving us with the chronic anticipation of betrayal as our dark and only beloved.

If we will only trust our mistrust, we will not know intimacy, but only a safeguarding that locks us out of our own depths. In such cancerous suspicion—an orange-alert of the psyche—we are eaten alive both inside and out. Yet even as we host paranoia, there still remains the possibility of turning toward it and going into its fearful core, until it is just endarkened feeling. Until we thus enter our fear, it will entrap us.

Turn not from your own turning away. Reach into that hobbled darkness, that psychic gutter, that grief crowded with rage, that poisoned shame, and reach in with open hand and outstretched heart, and what is in there will eventually come to you all unfisted and vulnerably bare, revealing itself to be not a problematic it, but rather reclaimed you.

Meet the hello already alive in every goodbye. As we launch our own odyssey into the Mystery not just of the transpersonal but also of the personal, no longer avoiding the sirensong of our own unique leanings, including those seemingly deranged instructors commonly known as obsessions, we discover that sometimes what works best is doing what doesn't work. The Mystery includes whatever attempts to figure out or explain It, thereby remaining unknowable—but not unlivable. We not only live It, but also live as It. Such is our freedom, from which there is no escape.

This unkempt precision, this wildly crystalline aesthetic, this seedling communication, this mad and multi-armed attempt of mine to somehow engage you and me beyond our rationality and cognitive strongholds—it depends so much on letting what is dumb, misshapen, lopsided, unattractive, immature, and seemingly crippled in me (and you) have enough space and light to add its unique gifts to my (and your) voicings.

Now this essay is trying to remember its beginning, wondering how the hell it got here from there. But does it really matter? Here we are, gathered from afar, each of us a spark of a waking star, fleshing out necessity, wandering half-blind through achingly real dreamlands, playing hide-and-seek with Divinity. So small we are, flickering for the briefest of moments, meteoric downswoops against the pure black of infinite space, and yet also so immeasurably vast are we, existing as more than we can possibly imagine.

CHAPTER 6

To Be Present

To be present is to consciously be here now, centered by Being—rather than by our egoity—without any recoil from our individuality. When we are present, we move from here to here, from now to now.

Being present dethrones our usual subjectivity—our self-obsessed, self-enclosed inwardness—leaving us with little or no allegiance to the viewpoint or intentions of our conditioning. Our underlying standpoint then becomes not *ours*, but Being's, however idiosyncratically colored or structured its actual *expression* might be. It's not that we become vacant or disengaged from our individuality, but that we cease, to a significant degree, letting our egoic self-sense center and represent us.

Being present decentralizes egoity.

But as natural as it is to be present, it's not our common state. More often than not, we are elsewhere and elsewhen, tangled up in past and future, dragging along yesterday as we hook ourselves to tomorrow. We may like the idea of being present, but we're generally not so fond of doing what it takes to be and remain present.

If we won't allow ourselves to be present when "we" don't want to be present, then we'll likely not get adequately acquainted with the us who does not give a damn about being present, the us that's adept at—and has a huge investment in—rationalizing and legitimizing our reactivity and mechanicalness.

It is difficult to be present when we have trouble or resist seeing our conditioning for what it is. Often, all that is actually present is our past, with its festering burden of unresolved hurt, numbing or amnesiac overlays, and compensatory addictions. Even those who have done considerable work on themselves may, when they know—or least have access to evidence—that they are far from present, *still* often act as if they indeed *are* present, fending off proof to the contrary, because openly admitting to such a "shortcoming" may be anathema to their spiritual status, as well as being just plain embarrassing.

How easy it is to fear, reject, or ignore signs that we are not where we think we should be, namely present, instead of simply becoming conscious of just who—or *what*—it is that has reduced being present to a credential, an ego-ornament. To thus evaluate ourselves is to diminish ourselves (whether through shrinkage or inflation), to degrade ourselves trying to make the grade.

When we slip, stumble, or fall, and then add insult to injury through indulging in self-deprecation, we need to discover who—or *what*—is generating such malignant critiquing, *without* getting caught up in judging our judging.

If we are genuinely committed to being present no matter what, then we will usually *welcome*—though not always initially!—those situations, inner or outer, which expose our faults and neurotic wanderings. The degree to which this occurs is the degree to which we've lost interest in looking good or spiritual.

Real spiritual opening is not some cleancut or antiseptic undertaking, but rather is an inherently messy undertaking, as intense, unpredictable, and *alive* as birth, eventually necessitating wholehearted entry into *everything* that we are, including what we despise about ourselves. The dirt cannot be avoided, and nor should it be. In fact, it needs to be appreciated and known without gloves, or else it will not become fitting soil for our emergence.

Trying to change the us who hasn't the slightest desire to get to the heart of the matter is not enough, though it may get things rolling. It is essential that we develop an unforced and real interest in that particular us, a curiosity and *compassion* that extends far beyond therapeutic and meditation chambers.

To thus explore our "downside"—our depressiveness, reactivity, violence, fear, cowardice, laziness—is not about our "up-ness" going slumming "down there", like some sort of obnoxiously sympathetic humanitarian or cultural superstar making the obligatory, praise-snaring rounds to the societally disadvantaged, but rather is about *descending* with Awakened feeling, and compassion into—and eventually through—what we have spent most of our life trying to rise above, subjugate, eviscerate, or forget. Here, we deliberately let ourselves be brought down, until there's no directional bias, but only *Being*, only reclaimed Self, only bare Presence.

Such intimacy with our ostracized aspects is not conceptually or symbolically arrived at. We cannot think or metaphorize our way through terror or dread. An essential step in working with such states is to—at the right time and at the right pace—move closer to them, to get *inside* them, while remaining present. This may be very unpleasant for a time, but it is ultimately liberating.

Being present does not always feel good. It is not about feeling good. In fact, it is not about feeling a particular feeling nor about feeling a particular way, and nor is it a matter of being in a particular circumstance. Being present simply means that *Being* is undeniably and significantly present, regardless of how it appears and feels.

So how do we get present?

First of all, by noticing and *openly* admitting when we are not or have not been present, or are only barely present. And how do we do that? By not treating our pain as an enemy or problem; by befriending our discomfort and failures; by ceasing to distract ourselves from our suffering; by no longer smothering our feelings of hopelessness with hope; and so on. And how, how do we do all this?

We can begin by not letting ourselves be seduced by the supposed sincerity of such questions, weaning ourselves not only from our superficial or merely curious questioning, but also from the unacknowledged *distancing* it provides. If we do so, the actual identity of the "questioner" sooner or later will be *nonconceptually* revealed. Sufficient attention must be freed from irrelevant concerns, or else Being will be reduced to just a bit of linguistic exotica.

We would also do well to not flee our hurt, nor use it as an excuse or bargaining device. Don't try to cure it, don't treat it as a problem or inconvenience or anomaly; instead, give it room to breathe and grieve and storm and unfurl and come fully alive, until it's not just yours, but *you*, reclaimed you.

To be present does not mean abiding with supposed awareness atop or "above" one's domesticated accumulations and pain. Indulging in such cerebral escapism is of no more value than is indulging in emotionalism, and is actually more dangerous, because its irrationality is far better camouflaged.

Be still.

Can you be still right now? Not just outwardly, but inwardly, too?

Has a minute passed, or only a few seconds? What is pulling your attention away from full participation in this moment? Where are you permitting your attention to go? And *whose* permission is it? Are you out of your mind, or are you informing yourself that I am? Is this a question to you, or something else?

Be still. And even stiller.

Real stillness does not necessarily require a cessation of movement or thought, but rather a relocation of attention to the actual process—and also the animating core—of movement and thought.

We don't have to be motionless to be present. In fact, we don't have to be anything in particular—all that is needed is to consciously *Be*.

There are so, so many enticing, compelling elsewheres and elsewhens clamoring for our consideration, but none of them need obstruct us. They are but attention-lures, nonproblematically encountered when we are present. Be stillness, Be movement, Be without trying to be other than what you are, Be so present that you have no conception of being present.

Being present Homes us.

CHAPTER 7

Spiritual Shortcuts

We are in such a hurry to get it, whatever it is. Gone into go. Greed for speed—fast food, fast money, fast relationships, fast spirituality. Drive-through divinity with fries and easy-to-swallow highs. Who wants to spend years doing spiritual practices when the same results apparently can—given a sufficiently open mind and wallet—be gained in just a weekend? We may even be told that all that can stop such a weekend from giving us the desired results is our belief that it cannot. And so the shearing of the sheep goes. Business as usual.

But the greater our hurry to arrive where we want to be spiritually, the longer it will take. What is spiritually greedy in us—if permitted to masquerade as us—weights us down as much as it revs us up, leaving us doing little more than spinning our wheels while we look around for better deals. But in true spiritual hunger, there is little or no wasting of time, which simultaneously means no hurry and no delay.

Spiritual shortcuts, like all shortcuts, are time-defined. But authentic spiritual practice does not *primarily* take place in time; if we say it takes a long time or a short time, we are only looking at it from the outside, tacking it down onto a straight time-calibrated measuring stick. When we are immersed in spirituality for real, we are not time-bound, even though we take care of business in a timely fashion.

The only spiritual shortcut is letting go of having any shortcut.

When we are sharing deep love with another, where does the time go? When we are really happy, where does the time go? It doesn't

29

go anywhere. Why? Because in such conditions it simply does not exist, except perhaps in a purely peripheral sense, and thus has nowhere to go. As we become more intimate with the Holy Deep, time—past, present, and future—becomes space, and space become Being.

Some may confuse Buddhism's Sudden School, as opposed to its Gradual School, of Enlightenment with a spiritual shortcut, but the Sudden School actually involves plenty of preparation for the "jump"—hence its symbiotic link with the Gradual School.

We'll pay so damned much for what we don't really need, and so little for what we really need. We want Freedom for free. A man once asked the Dalai Lama how he could more quickly get to Enlightenment, and the Dalai Lama reportedly wept for him, recognizing how much pain that man must be in to want to get to the big E faster. We think that getting it spiritually will give us immunity from pain and all the troublesome stuff of life—what a fantasy! Spirituality ultimately means no escape, no need for escape, and utter freedom *through* limitation and every sort of difficulty.

Shortcuts are time-framed. Short time, long time, etcetera. But Awakening is not time-framed. Being occurs not in time, but in Timelessness. So even to want a spiritual shortcut is but a confession of estrangement from Being.

When the desire to access such a shortcut arises, enter the very feeling of the desire, bypassing its mind, until you are at its core, pressed against its primal pulse. Then let your attention pass through that core-feeling, that primordial ache, until it rests in the feeling of Being. Do so, and notice how your flesh becomes but patterned energy, wearing nothing but the attention given it. No wristwatch. No clock on the wall—and not just because there's no wall, but also because there's no one needing there to be a clock. That in us which functions through time can, of course, continue, but it cannot now masquerade as us. In fact, nothing can.

Gotta run. Busy day ahead. A pain in the ass, but kind of intoxicating, isn't it, keeping us so damned busy that the mysteries of the obvious go all but unnoticed. But still something gets through the cracks in our amphetamine days, making light of our dreams, asking only for our undivided attention, our time. The door is, as always, already open, even as we do battle over who has the right key. Awakening, we smile with huge compassion upon what we've done with our time. The hourglass catches our glance, spinning into a flaming mandala of spilling forms, leaving a timeless clearing that is everywhere at once, inhabited by a gratitude of which these words are but the feeblest echo.

CHAPTER 8

Groundlessness
& the Dark Night

We crave solidity when we lack ground. We understandably get very attached to what seems to root or reassuringly secure us.

But if we are to find a truer ground, we will have to endure being uprooted. This means that we, for an unspecified time, will have to experience groundlessness, a free-floating, treacherously contoured, mapless zone that is more like a gap than a locale.

This gap, this no-one's-land, this amorphous and maddeningly blurry clearing, is horizontally elastic, stretched out between past and future, and is vertically without boundaries. We can rise and fall in it until there is no up and down, but only pure centerless openness. Or we can rise and fall in it until we are so desperate for clearcut direction and steady footing that we make ourselves overly susceptible to whatever or whomever convincingly promises us unambiguous direction and solid ground.

We all experience tiny moments of groundlessness every day, if only during almost immediately forgotten thoughts and intimations, but sooner or later we encounter not-so-tiny moments of groundlessness, from which we cannot easily distract ourselves. Then, though there may be considerable fear or despair or depression, we have an opportunity to go not back to where we were before, but rather into a depth of Being that we could before only visit for the briefest of moments.

The gateway to this depth is so narrow that we cannot pass through it if we insist on bringing the luggage of our past with us. Everyday groundlessness only makes us cling more tightly to our past and the sense of familiarity that it brings, but existential groundlessness—wherein it seems that *everything*, including our very identity, is up for questioning—loosens our grasp on the familiar, potentially leaving us so raw and uncertain that we are opened to the unimaginable depth of Being right before us.

This is not to say that this is easy. In fact, it may the most difficult passage of our life. Before the gate opens for us, there may fall a darkness like we have never known, which St. John of the Cross famously called the Dark Night of the Soul. Getting stuck in birthing canals can be remarkably hellish. Great doubt may arise during the Dark Night. Let it. Watch your mind madly churn and propagandize, while you anchor your attention to the underlying feelings and sensations. Hope may flutter like a spectral flag, tattered beyond repair. Let it. Give hope the opportunity to give up the ghost, so that faith—which is to the present as hope is to the future—may deepen. Doubt your doubt. Don't expect anything to make sense. Open, and keeping opening, to what is more real than meaning. Endure until you can wait without waiting. Shift from having faith in the solidity of things to having faith in Being.

In the Dark Night, we may feel an intensity of despair, fear, and depressiveness that seems intolerable. Yet as we learn to bear the unbearable, we gradually settle into the darkness, sensing not only its heaviness and lack of light, but also its fertility. Seeds grow in the dark. So do we.

CHAPTER 9

Keeping in Touch
When We're Out of Touch

The closer we are, the more painful the absence of closeness between us.

A feeling of disconnection arises, the mind makes lists of reasons why, attention gauges the density and strength of the barrier between us. Something in me says "oh shit!" and something else in me says "this too"—voices of alarm and voices of acceptance simultaneously ricocheting through me. The witness is present, but love is having trouble taking root. Stormwinds make it difficult. What's left of me cannot see a way out—except maybe intellectually—but there's a knowing, without thinking, that the way out is in.

Being close to you, really close, feels so good, so heartwarming and nourishing, that it's easy to make a problem out of times when I don't feel close to you. What I tell myself at these times I have learned to not take very seriously, for it is mostly just the voice of self-importance in reactive headgear.

My challenge, my ongoing labor of love, is to be intimate with whatever is occurring, including my and your closed-off-ness. It is, of course, easier to spot yours, and to hold it accountable for mine. Why this is not funnier simply highlights my stuckness. It's not so easy to be intimate with the difficult stuff within when we are actually in it up to our eyeballs. But after a certain point—the length of which is an accurate measure of self-inflicted suffering—what else is there to do? How much longer do I want to grind away at this consistently unsatisfying waltz of avoidance? How much more can I milk it for it's-not-fair handouts?

Being intimate with the difficult stuff is not about feel-good payoffs, but about not losing touch with what really matters, however fragile or slippery our connection to that may be. Spending some conscious, present-moment time openly feeling—feeling into, feeling through, feeling for—my closed-off-ness to you opens me, if only by widening the cracks in whatever self-obsessed containers I am busy occupying. Not so easy this is, given that I am likely not feeling very much like taking a break from my funk or whatever else is so fucking important that I've let it possess me.

But when I'm in the muck—caught up in feeling bad about my relationship with you—I can at least acknowledge that that is where I am, however embarrassing it might be to me. This is where I can very profitably drop all blame, and stop indulging in reactivity and also in any self-condemnation for being reactive.

Drop all romantic notions of what conscious relationship means—unpleasantries will continue to happen, reactivity will keep showing up, stupidities large and small will continue to cross our path, and thank God for this, for without it we would very likely stay asleep, too snuggled in to our waking slumber to rub the sleep out of our I's. Gratitude in the revelatory raw this is, gratitude for what we "normally" do not feel any gratitude. What gets us back on track? Sometimes making and taking enough time to let what's happened settle. Sometimes letting another's pain really touch us. Mostly, though, it is a matter of becoming more present. Even if we are in a seriously endarkened state, we can be present in it and to it, and we can also remember to love.

This does not mean that our heart will necessarily open very easily, but it does mean that a seed of awakening is being nourished. What else can we do when we are off track, and recognize that this is so, other than locate and nourish our intention to get back on track? As we lift our heads from the mud, we are akin to the first creatures that left the sea and found themselves on land, wriggling free enough of their past to take in the sky.

So many clouds, shapeshifting, coming and going, long-lasting and short-lasting, silver and black and creamy and drenched in fiery splendor, cloud after cloud, all passing through achingly pure sky. We are that sky, home to all of our qualities, embracing both thunderbolt and ethereal wisp, already having room for all, already being both all and more than all, already beyond grasping and understanding, yet always right here, reminding us when we are clouded by difficulties that whatever is happening is only part of what is really happening.

This we cannot truly figure out or explain, but only embrace, letting it remind us of our original face, the one we had before time began. Thus do we expand our love. Thus do we touch what has always touched us. Thus do we go on, gradually lessening our demand that our path be straight, until we are not only walking Awakening's pathless path, but are that path. Thus do we become what we seek. This is not the end, but the beginning.

CHAPTER 10

Suffering Versus Pain

Though pain and suffering are often thought of as being much the same, they differ greatly from each other.

Pain is fundamentally just unpleasant sensation. Suffering, on the other hand, is something we are *doing* with our pain. Pain comes, often inescapably so, with life. It often also is, especially in its awakening or alerting capacity, necessary. Suffering, however, is far less necessary than we might think.

When we cannot sufficiently distract or distance ourselves from our pain, we generally turn it into suffering. How? By overdramatizing our pain. We make an unpleasantly gripping story out of it, a tale in which our hurt "I" all but automatically assumes the throne of self. I hurt, therefore I am—this is suffering's core credo.

In so doing, we are simply *identifying* with our pain, overpersonalizing it.

Where pain is consciously felt hurt, suffering is the manipulation of that hurt into drama, wherein we're likely so busy acting out—and being literally *occupied* by—our hurt role that we've little or no motivation to stand apart from it.

In the myopic theatrics of suffering, pain itself mostly just stagnates, like an unwanted exhibit in an art gallery. It is not really touched. As the centerpiece and supposed raison d'être of suffering, pain is kept from any genuine healing. We may feel close to our pain when we are busy suffering, but it is not the kind of closeness that heals. It is, in fact, an

37

unwelcome proximity, through which we generally just reinforce our suffering, if only because of our sheer desperation to be elsewhere (like in some kind of fantasized immunity from pain, or similar dreamland of our suffering-centered "I").

The degree to which we turn our pain into suffering is the degree to which we obstruct our own healing.

When we're busy suffering, we are all but bereft of healthy detachment. We're then removed from the naked reality of our pain—for our attention is generally more on our storyline than on the raw, nonconceptual sense of our pain—but not removed in a way that permits us to focus more clearly on what is actually going on.

As such, suffering is unhealthy separation from our pain. Suffering is pain that's gone to mind, pain that's doing time in mental cells, mental hells.

The more intimate we are with our pain, the less we suffer.

To work effectively with our suffering, we need both to stand apart from its script and to cease distancing ourselves from our pain. Suffering may seem to keep us near to our pain, but it actually keeps us from getting as close to our pain as we need to, if we are live a more liberated life.

Suffering houses pain, but keeps it in the dark. When we turn on the lights, the dramatics of suffering become transparent. Then the uncensored facticity of our pain gets our full attention, particularly at the level where it is but unpleasant sensation. Then we can enter our pain with care, clarity, and precision, getting to know it from the *inside*—its fluxing weave and interplay of shape, color, temperature, texture, directionality, intensity, pressure, location, layering, and so on.

Often when we say we're in pain, we're not really *in* our pain, but rather are only closer to it than we'd like. But in fact, we're still *outside* it.

It is in the conscious and caring entry *into* our pain that we begin to find some real freedom from our pain. The hurt may remain, but our relationship to that hurt will have changed to the point where it's no longer such a problem to us, and in fact may even become a doorway into What-Really-Matters.

The healing of pain is found *in* pain itself.

As we become more *intimate* with our pain, we find that we are less troubled by it. Suffering is, among other things, a refusal to develop any intimacy with our pain. In fact, suffering only jails our pain.

But the cage door is open, already open, as we'll see if we just turn around, away from the screens upon which our suffering projects its stories. Then we begin to awaken, to exit our entrapping dreams. Awareness upstages suffering, dissolving its grip on us, taking us to the heart, the core, the epicenter, of our pain.

And there, in that place of hurt, we meet not more hurt, but more us. More healing, more peace, more sacred welcome.

CHAPTER 11

The Blows are Not the Problem

Only in the dreamy flatlands of cinematic confections do the heavy blows of life not fall. But in actuality they fall to all, privileged and destitute alike. It may seem to us that some get off easy, but that is simply because another's suffering may not always look like suffering to us.

What are the blows? Are they fate, karma, destiny, or just crappy luck? We may never absolutely know, but we do know, sooner or later, that all we really can do is make the best possible use of them. What else is there to do? The blows are a given. Some may prove beneficial relatively quickly, especially if we take them as opportunities. But others, even when wholeheartedly related to as opportunities, may show little or no benefit for a long time, maybe even a lifetime. No guarantees.

The fact that more blows are coming, and will keep on coming, is not necessarily bad news, but rather just one of Life's givens, asking for a nonproblematic response—not so easy, but definitely possible. Our task is not to find some kind of immunity from blows, but rather is to learn to relate *to* each blow, to skillfully coexist and work—and ultimately flow—with it.

This is not about *submission*—which would mean being unresistingly enslaved and diminished by the pressures and impact of a blow—but rather is about *surrender*, a conscious, dynamic acceptance of the *essential* energies of a blow, which enables us to simultaneously ride and be swept along by it, in much the same spirit that we might successfully bodysurf a massive wave. We are out of control and yet simultaneously

40

are not. Instead of just fighting the wave or letting it crush us—as in submitting to it—we *blend* with it, entering an intimacy with it that enriches and deepens us, an intimacy that ensures we will not lose touch with what really matters.

Blows can radically alter our life course. That's part of what we fear about them. We may think we're okay with being out on our edge, but when we are actually knocked way out of our comfort zones, we generally get very distressed. We finally find him or her, then he or she leaves, changes too much, dies. Just when we get cozy in our new home, a lawsuit shows up that threatens to take it all away. But it's all going to be taken away, anyway—and we might as well be prepared well beforehand. In his early 50s, the Dalai Lama was asked what he was going to do with the rest of his life, and he replied, "Prepare for my death." He wasn't being morbid. He was being practical, straightforward. Nothing heavy about it. Yes, we all know we are going to die, but he *really* knows it. If we really knew it, we wouldn't be so unprepared for our death, which, of course, can arrive any time. And nor would we be so unprepared for the blows that are coming—yes, we might still be knocked flat, but we would not be so flattened, nor so down about being down.

So the blows can be taken as a kind of training. If we react, and continue reacting, badly to them, acting as if we are no more than victims, then we get to stay stuck, small, childish, centered by blame. However, if we choose to take the blows as training opportunities—to whatever degree—we increase our odds of awakening to what we truly are.

Without awakening thus, Life is little more than a nightmare, sometimes an airbrushed, ultracozy, or anesthetized nightmare, but nonetheless still a nightmare, a knotted ball of self-enclosed melodrama bouncing around in artificially lit darkness. Without awakening from the entrapping dreams we chronically animate—and is there any dream that is not ultimately entrapping?—there is no real freedom. If we were utterly satisfied with our life, never disappointed or disillusioned, we would then have no impetus to wake up; we could just keep on dreaming, so lost in mind-realms that we would have no inkling that we were thus lost. So be grateful that Life has such power to disappoint and disillusion us.

When small blows do not do the job, larger blows often make an appearance, attracted by our need—our more often than not insufficiently recognized need—to be liberated from our delusions and their trappings. Large blows may seem unfair, especially when we've been good for a long time—but maybe then we're just all the more ready to make wise use of such blows. Do we get more pain that we can handle? Sometimes. But eventually—eventually—we can work with it, if we keep cultivating a willingness to do so. Just because we cannot handle a blow when it arrives, or even for some time after, does not necessarily mean that we will never be able to handle it.

Blows anger us, flatten us, shame us, inconvenience and injure us. When they arrive, we may feel shock, anger, shame, fear, in no particular order and all in a short time. Our mind may whip through a bunch of scenarios, mostly disastrous to us, until we shift our attention to the bare reality of our feelings. Then we start to settle, eventually finding that we have more room than we thought for our upsetting circumstance and its possible consequences. We're not necessarily happy about it, but we start to feel more peace. Perhaps we may be in danger of losing much of what we have, but now can recognize that if we have to lose it or let it go, then we might as well be prepared. This is not negative thinking, but simply readiness. So we practice opening to and relaxing into this readiness. Not knowing the outcome of our upsetting circumstance can be an occasion for worry and anxiety, or it can be an occasion for settling more deeply into Being. It's up to us.

Being sued, being left, being lied to, being betrayed, being humiliated, being treated like a non-entity—the list goes on and on—all need to be divested of their dramatics so that they can be seen as the raw ride that they are. But what if we cannot ride them? Then do what it takes to be their pasture, their wilderness, their sky.

Practice with the little blows, the inevitable pain-in-the-ass moments that punctuate most days for just about all of us. Then, when the big blows come, they still blow us away, but not for so long—when we gather our breath, and find some ground, we will find the situation workable, at least spiritually.

Blows may deposit us where we would rather not be, but how are we to truly know what the most conducive conditions are for our awakening? Getting all tied up in a mind-knot about how much a lawsuit may cost us only strands us from our being. Freedom does not mind blows. Freedom does not mind its chains.

Freedom is to misfortune as the sky is to its clouds; it holds misfortune with great care and tenderness, but without framing it as a tragedy or a raw deal. Freedom may weep for misfortune's pain, but it is not diminished by its weeping. In fact, the grief that signals surrender to a blow carries us, sooner or later, into a spaciousness that is none other than undressed Freedom.

Blows can catalyze compassion—now we can really feel what it is like for others in a similar position to us. And we're all fundamentally in the same position, regardless of where we are stationed on the boat. The captain may be more protected from the storm than the deckhand, but not for long. When we realize with our whole being that we are all on the Titanic, then what could be more appropriate than compassion and mutual support in embodying that depth of Being that outlives us?

Don't let blows embitter you. Don't let them dishearten you. Be ready for them the way you are ready for your next inhalation. Worry and anxiety are not readiness, but only tempests in a me-knot. Cultivating a relaxed alertness is readiness. Practice it whenever you can, so that when you are knocked off your feet—as you inevitably will be, from time to time—you don't take long to recall and reenter such practice, even as you shake with rage or fear or shock. Soften without losing your spine or dignity. Love as though Death could arrive at any time. Die into a truer Life. No maps—we know the way by heart.

CHAPTER 12

Behead Your Hope

Hope is surrogate faith, faith so uprooted from the here-and-now that it has put all its bets on tomorrow. Hope is pothead optimism, stoned on possibility. Hope is little more than despair taking a crash course in positive thinking.

Regardless of its vigorously scrubbed smile, however, hope is not much more than unhappiness scavenging for distraction and consolation, and what better place to do that than the future? Hope is nice, cleancut seduction, smelling more of apple pie than of bordello chambers. Even so, its narcotic power should not be underestimated.

Hope is a storybook romance with Later. Its promises only lure us into postponing being fully here now, greening our deserts with peptalk oases and plastic shade trees.

Where hope promises, faith gives. Where hope dreams, faith awakens. Where hope seduces, faith loves. Hope fantasizes about which way to go. Faith knows the way by heart. Letting go of hope and its hyperfocus on tomorrow deepens our faith.

When we allow ourselves to see everything—*everything*—as already dying, already returning to its source, and when we do so without fleeing our attachment or polluting our heart's aching with hope, we enter a depth of Life in which disappointment no longer disappoints us and death no longer deadens us.

Behead your hope. Do not permit possibility to seduce you. Adapt to the climate of the present, no matter how strongly bad weather makes you nostalgic for the future.

Whatever we have is already dying, already seeded with its nonexistence, even as we keep trying to rejuvenate and perpetuate it. As we sublime our sorrow over this into pure grief—perhaps after passing through some raging preliminaries—we bring dignity to our helplessness, compassion to our failures, humor to our doubt, and a sobering happiness to our labor.

Injustice, misfortune, shitty circumstances—in facing these with an uncluttered mind, unshuttered heart, and untight belly, we make room for wise responses to emerge.

We are never truly abandoned.

Consider betrayal by an intimate—the sting and shock and stabbing hurt of it can easily convince us that we've been abandoned. We're so overwhelmed with pain that we permit ourselves to be governed by the thoughts that arise from and reinforce it, thereby losing ourselves in the darkly compelling dramatics of betrayal. However, given that betrayal is often inevitable—and perhaps even necessary, in ways usually not obvious at the time—we would be wise not to attempt to minimize the possibility of its occurrence through avoiding real intimacy. We can use the very wound of betrayal, the cut and burn and violence of it, to widen and deepen our receptivity to that which can never abandon us.

However difficult it can be, our life provides a remarkable opportunity, for consistently present in it is everything that we need to reawaken to What-Really-Matters. How could we thus reawaken if there were no convincingly solid, sense-binding, fittingly populated theater in which to directly experience—and therefore learn from—the consequences of what we are making of ourselves?

Behead your hope. As we open to the disillusionment-possibilities that Life offers, we recognize the sharply etched, viscerally eloquent feedback of pain, learning to see through its density and to unzip its dramatics, becoming more conscious of how we literally dream ourselves into being this, that, or the other.

Slumbering Buddhas are we all, needing only to rub the sleep out of our I's. As we recognize our disguise, we find ourselves being Awakened by all things.

Go beyond hope. Stop flirting with possibility. Hope is but suffering drunk on nicely smiling forecasts, romancing us with sunny tomorrows, uprooting and stranding us from the present moment. Hope is nostalgia for the future.

Hope has not the radical trust that real faith embodies, but it can transmute into such faith, if we will but behead it. Taking the mind out of hope brings us to our senses, giving us the guts and ground to take fitting action. Instead of just hoping for a better tomorrow, we then enter into *doing* what has to be done to make a better now, and in so doing prepare the soil for a better tomorrow. Then we simply pick up the shovel, thinking not shit but compost, not tomorrow but now, exactly now. It's in our hands.

CHAPTER 13

Riding a Wave
of Everlasting Morning

Lone eagle drifting so high across milky lapis sky, floating like an escaped dream, riding a wave of everlasting morning.

Life, and a deeper Life— such an infinitely variegated arising, intoxicatingly intimate with its beginningless Beginning, its ungraspable Truth. So much to say about what cannot be said. The eagle is long gone, but can still be spotted somewhere behind the eyes, the sunburnt mahogany of its feathers glistening with cerebrospinal fluid.

The specific blooms best when it keeps in touch with its ancestry, its nondual roots. We all have been singled out, crystallized into uniqueness. It's so easy to personalize this, making a self out of our particulars, dreaming that we are not dreaming. Such is our density.

When things get very real, vividly and mind-transcendingly real, we'll often say that they feel unreal or dreamlike. The felt transparency and constant fluxing of the seemingly solid undoes our apparent solidity. What happens to dream-beings who realize they are dreaming? What remains?

Nothing is new. Everything is new. Since both are true, what will you do? Life only makes sense when we stop trying to make it make sense.

Ragged shadows millimeter across the lawn. Children who will not play here for decades now stand here barefooted and achingly aswirl, just like these words straining against their linguistic limitations, trying to decipher the wordless whisperings of their shredded birthsac.

The day grows choppier. Cerebral rafts capsize, wrinkles multiply. We fortify ourselves with stuff, making a virtue out of accumulation, including the spiritual Brownie points we tack up behind our forehead.

However, when we get right down to it, we discover that subtraction may be more fundamental than addition—recognizing and embodying our true destiny is mostly an eliminatory undertaking, an ever deeper letting go. We lose it all to *be* it all. We are always being invited to make windows for the Invisible, until our frames no longer bind nor blind us, until we are nothing but window, an unbound clearing or openness with room for all.

Lone eagle's ghost paling across fracturing eggshell skies, leaving a snowy jet-trail, a faint thread of remembrance, its stranding suddenly thickly veined and bloody-blue and wound through the Minotaur's suckling cries, our everyday lies, our aborted goodbyes. Now the shadows are embroidered with birdsong. The poignancy of the particular, the mortal, the personal, finds its deepest appreciation and translation in the heart of Being.

The broken heart opens us to unbroken Being. And then there is only Love. Only What-Really-Matters. Only God. What does all this mean? God only knows.

Little word-houses, crammed with recycled selfing and a staggering complexity of inlaid overlapping forces. Metaphor must bow to its preconceptual roots, if it is to avoid being enlisted in the service of disembodied rationality. Before there were archetypes, there was naked Wonder. Before there was meaning, there was significance. Before there was you, there was…

Clouds spreadeagle the sky. The familiar fades. The wind fingers the shadows. Shafts of light gut the clouds. A bottomless connection floods the highlands. Unimaginable intimations swim by, making more than sky and less than a self. Other worlds beckon, then fade as my step bypasses them, already feeling the coming rain.

Information falls down speechless before Truth. The wind, green and sharp, has picked up, drowning out the campaigning of my mind for hasty reelection. Beauty breaks free of its cellophane and framing. The usual us is just a thought away.

The sky is bluish silver, bruised and bulging with rain. The firs and pines and weeds sway orgasmically in the fennel-stained breeze, pulling me into their exquisitely timed timeless dance, their everyday primordial trance. Everything is pulsing and everything is still. A moving motionlessness. And here we are, gathered from afar, wiping away the last traces of these words, at home with our every feeling, already inside our inside, already outside welcoming the rain, the sweet hard rain, letting ourselves be lived, with compassionate daring and unobstructed caring. Letting all the worlds emerge from and as us.

Lone eagle drifting so high across milky lapis sky, floating like an escaped dream, riding a wave of everlasting morning.

Hello to the you who's here, and hello to the you who's still arriving.

Welcome Home.

CHAPTER 14

What's Right About
What's Wrong in Relationships

We want so damn badly to get it right in our relationships, as evidenced by all the books and television shows on how to have better relationships, all the songs of heartache and break and mend, all the hunting and hoping and groping for that special somebody who'll do right by us, all the efforting, manipulation, self-marketing, and strategizing to get it right, to get it to last, to get it to satisfy—all sentenced to the labor of making us feel better or at least more secure, consuming more of our attention and energy than we'd bargained for, leaving us burdened and bewildered and close to not much more than depression and burnout, yet still hot-wired to enough paint-by-numbers advice to be marooned from the fact that real relationship, relationship rooted in love and a mutual commitment to waking up, is not only less nice and more challenging than we thought, but also more *messy* (like this sentence).

Sometimes intimate relationship can be such a drag, such a high maintenance hassle, such a drain, knocking us around until we swear we'll not reenter such a hazardous arena, regardless of its goodies. But it usually doesn't take much time for us to jump back in again, high on hope (as when we get a tidbit of unexpected openness from an emotionally stingy partner). Maybe we will do better this time; maybe we'll meet someone who won't screw us around; maybe we'll handle it better. Such melodrama, such endlessly rich material this is for stand-up comedy, soap operas, and everyday gossip. And for something deeper, too, as we shall see.

Sloppy dialogue, emotional illiteracy, go-nowhere arguments, little cruelties, everyday stupidities, mismatched desires, mechanical rituals, halfheartedness, putting off what needs to be done—these are some of the things that clutter relationships. They resist the vacuuming of good intentions. They resist both rational persuasion and emotional pleas. They go wherever we go, following us into and out of our dreams. At essence, they are just longtime habits tracking mud and worse into our shared space, while masquerading as us. It's so messy, no matter how well-scrubbed our place and face is.

But in the messiness of a conscious relationship, such habits become nakedly *obvious*, clashing and colluding with each other before a mutually knowing eye, clearly needing more than a laundry spin, more than a communications course, more than better table manners. Such habits have gotten away with referring to themselves as us, but now cannot do so for long, as we, more and more, relate *to*, rather than *from*, them.

Intimate relationship not only includes the mingling and encounter of differences, but also inevitably catalyzes a blatant *exaggeration* or flaring-up of differences, a vividly dramatized exposure—however unwittingly animated!—of all sorts of oppositions, difficult mixes, impasses, and *overdefended* positionings that would have otherwise very likely remained more camouflaged or untouched.

As unpleasant as this might feel—and the worse it feels, the more valuable it probably is—it signals a great opportunity to know ourselves more fully, because so much of what needs to be worked through for our own maturation is right before us, literally outfront.

Relationship thus provides an environment, both outer and inner, wherein what we don't like or don't want to know—or don't know—about ourselves is given center stage, just like in a dream. And there we may stand or stumble, seemingly transfixed by the spotlight, held in place both by our attachment to the other and to our own ideologies, feeling the heat of our preferences starting to flame into reactivity.

This point, where we typically would trot out our usual roles—the misunderstood one, the victim, the reasonable one, etcetera—is precisely where even a trace of wakefulness is of immense use, to inwardly acknowledge not only our state, but also the degree of our *identification* with that state. When a mutually compassionate eye can be cast upon the highlighted reactivity of one or both partners, the relationship is on course.

> *The deeper you and I do dive*
> *The less we mind upsetting waves*
> *Embracing the roughness of wild seas*
> *We touch and are touched by a sobering joy*
> *Giving each other the freedom to be*
> *Exactly where we are*
> *I love this climb with you, this ride, this opening*
> *This stumbling and soaring, this deep sharing*
> *Willingly, gratefully, trustingly I walk, leap, plunge*
> *Into the succulent crucible of your love and laughter*
>   *and invitation to find freedom through our shared heart,*
>   *our shared body, our shared limitations, our shared boundlessness,*
>   *our shared being, our shared YES!*

But as good as it gets, intimate relationship still can be a two-headed hell-raiser. There are times when the shared heart is split into two densely-walled camps; there are times when the shared body is a vacant lump; there are times when the shared limitations are just a royal pain in the shared ass; there are times when the shared boundlessness is just an idea; there are times when the shared being is crowded with loneliness; there are times when the shared yes is riddled with doubt. Such times are fierce teachers, testers and potential deepeners of our faith, inviting us to get back on track.

When we are intimate with an other, we can be very, very hurt. We can become crazily jealous, possessive, obsessed, angry in ways we never thought possible, our spiritual practices shredding into near nonexistence in the storms of our pain and reactivity. It might seem under such conditions that our capacity for awakening has been severely diminished, but that is from the viewpoint that sees only the turbulence, the chaos, the unpleasantness of what is happening. However, in such rough and wild waters swirls another possibility, one equipped with nothing but a lifeline to our heartland. If we take hold of it, we start to recognize what's right about what's wrong; we treat the shit as compost; we let the pain tear open our heart; we learn to love when we are not being loved or don't feel loved.

However, if we only try to *think* our way through our relationship hassle, we merely confine its turbulent forces in our minds, thereby intensifying our *confusion*, instead of letting such forces *fuel* our leap into a more fitting level of being. Here, we recognize and treat relational intimacy not as an end, but rather as a *means*, an extremely potent crucible for Awakening's alchemy.

> *Tired we fight then stop caring about who's right*
> *Together touching an aching*
> *That gives us enough heart to see*
> *What's right about what's wrong*
> *We settle into the evernew familiarity*
> *Of the everdeep, moving closer*
> *To perpetual perishing's bare beauty*
> *And the daily grind's tiny treasures*
> *We get more comfortable with the uncomfortable*
> *Including the fear of being so close*
> *That even the smallest unkindness*
> *Stabs, smacks, squeezes the life out of the heart*
> *But, but do not our wounds*
> *When held with awakened care*
> *Plunge us naked into the Sacred?*
> *So let's include in our embrace*
> *All of it, every pain and joy, every up and down*
> *Every bit of sun and rain, every loss and gain*
> *So short this time to be together*
> *Yet it's time enough to reenter the timeless*
> *The day's tasks call and pull and drag*
> *Summer floats by the window like an escaped dream*

While we make shopping lists and forget to breathe
Now everything's out on the dancefloor
Wallflowers suddenly in bloom
So much space here
Room for all

There's nothing like an intimate relationship to let us know that we're not as developed as we thought. We may, in meditative retreat or metaphysical flight, assume without much challenge that we are sitting with our less-than-admirable qualities, being mindful of them, etcetera, but real relationship does not waste much time in letting us know the difference between sitting *with* such qualities and sitting *on* them.

Being in such relationship is generally a rude awakening. It steps on the toes of our egoity, unimpressed by our credentials, drawing us into a dharma drama in which our neuroses initially get to star as us, and then are divested of such pretension, becoming but grist for the mill of Awakening. To the degree that we are attached to our egoity and neurotic rituals, a real relationship will, more often than not, seem like just one insult after another.

The sooner we ask what's right about what's wrong in our relationships, the sooner we'll discover the real value and purpose of them.

This may mean approaching our relationships in ways to which we are not accustomed. Sometimes being off our path is our path. Sometimes what works best is to spend some time in what doesn't work. Watching the worst of television, as an alternative to meditation and prayer, can be good medicine for spiritual constipation. We can get so busy trying to be good, trying to stay on the path, trying to be a successful somebody in a conscious relationship, that we stagnate, barely able to move beneath the sheer weight of all our documented failures. Making more room for our intimate relationship to sometimes be messy—which does not mean making a virtue out of laziness and inconsiderateness—helps keep it clean, undirtied by purity.

This does not, however, necessarily mean clear sailing. Any relationship can trigger us. Good relationships trigger the hell out of us without trashing the relationship; great relationships trigger the hell out of us while deepening the relationship. And the best relationships use whatever happens, however hellish or disheartening, not only to deepen the relationship, but to also awaken us beyond it.

What doesn't work in a relationship is what can make it truly work—especially in the sense of giving us sufficient jolts to alert us to our trances, consensual and otherwise—but only if such difficulties are dealt with not as problems, but as opportunities. Not easy, not easy at all. After all, this asks that we venture from the shoreline into some really big waves.

We may like thinking about how great it is to be at our edge—which is where growth occurs—but actually being there is not necessarily much of a picnic. In fact, it may be so damned unpleasant, so scary, so hard to stomach, that we find some convincing alibis to do otherwise—such as literally leaving the relationship, withdrawing from it while still in it, or keeping it relatively superficial.

(About leaving a relationship: First of all, there is no inherent virtue in staying. What matters is that we do not leave prematurely. Hanging in there when it is rough or unnourishing or pointless is just as important as leaving when it has been rough or unnourishing or pointless for too long. We have to ask ourselves—and *not* when we are busy being reactive or close-hearted!—if we are truly being served or furthered by the relationship: Are the difficulties therein challenging us in a way that we need to be challenged, or are they simply eroding us? If the answer to this varies according to our mood, it's not the answer.)

We cannot connect unless we are already separate; and we cannot separate unless we are already connected. Such is the apparent paradox of relationship. Real intimacy is the art of balancing togetherness and apartness, so that they are not so much polar opposites as they are dance partners. The relationship is the dancefloor; what we don't like about each other and ourselves the wallflowers; and the music and movement Life Itself, at once outlasting us and appearing as us.

In the liberating bondage of real intimacy, our separateness is not a problem, but rather a ticket Home, providing more than enough grist for the mill of Awakening.

Part of what makes a relationship truly rewarding is an ongoing mutual intimacy with what doesn't work in the relationship.

The obstacles we encounter in relationship are not really obstacles, but catalysts in drag. Catalysts for what? For waking up. Be grateful to have someone so close to you who can so easily push your buttons—and maybe even install a few. It's not so easy to stay buttoned-up when we're in close to another. Healthy relationships don't let us remain intact, cool, immune. They kick our mutual butt so hard that we can't sit for long on our stuff. How infuriating, how inconvenient, what a pain in the ass! And what a gift.

And what a joy—to enter so deeply into shared living that *everything* is permitted to awaken us. And to be so close, so attached, that we cannot get away for very long from the inevitable challenges of such relationship. This is freedom, freedom through limitation, freedom through traveling together no matter what the weather.

Freedom through intimacy.

CHAPTER 15

The Dream's Petals
Cradle Many a Viewfinder

The dream's petals cradle many a viewfinder.

Like disembodied gypsies, like midnight breezes restlessly adrift, like nothing in particular, a few thoughts wander through old rooms, trying to snare some attention, drumming up a dream. The feeling is that of spectral undersea ruins, lump-headed eels necking out of broken hulls like huge fanged grubs. But the threat does not run deep. Everything seems absorbable, permeable, edible, vividly different yet strangely similar, solidified by my step.

The dream gathers more focus, and an unknown woman soundlessly floats toward me. The floor's a patchwork, a fractured chessboard seemingly on the verge of rolling up. The woman has only one eye, in-between and slightly above where her eyebrows ought to be. She starts to leave, then spins around, pushing an immense solid metal box onto me. Quickly I step back, peculiarly unalarmed, and sit down cross-legged with my eyes lightly closed, waiting to be crushed, yet knowing I cannot be harmed. The dream vanishes. So do I.

So many rooms, so many dark and winding trails, the living and the dead so closely intertwined. And so many here yet already gone, refusing to give up the ghost. Dreams are what seem real when we are asleep. Is any thing really more real than a dream? To say it's all a dream is no consolation whatsoever. No "I" can stand apart from it all so as to realize that it's all a dream, for every "I" is itself but dreamstuff, regardless of its beliefs about itself and reality.

We talk of making up our mind, but we mostly just let our mind make us up. An entrancing fiction is the result, so convincingly personified that we take it to be us.

Our innocence doesn't easily outgrow its naiveté. Blinders come with the operational manual for incarnation. The whispers of other worlds get lost in the hustle and muscle of our overdeveloped concerns. Our romancing of tomorrow ties us to yesterday. Nothing lasts the way we want it to. Whether or not we have what we want, we still experience pain. Worse, we continue dramatizing our pain, thereby turning it into suffering, while addicting ourselves to whatever most pleasurably or potently distracts us from our suffering.

What we refuse to face festers and multiplies within us—and also around us, as if magnetically drawn to us—until it literally takes our place, looking through our eyes and harnessing our energies to its own ends. This isn't necessarily the possession of horror films or voodooistic rites, but it is still possession.

What we suppress suppresses us.

Nevertheless, the opportunity remains the same. The bazaar smokily comes into view, its thousand chattering arms claiming our streets, its raucously clattering wares hauling in our eyes and appetites, its ancient voices calling us by names we've forgotten but not completely forgotten. Chickens run around in swaying wooden cages, their squawks barely heard, their already-torn heads waiting for the axe. Medicinal roots hang against the back walls of dusty stalls, their smell at once pungent and sweetly inviting, packed with labyrinthine power.

Chew on this. Bite into it. Let its bitter aromatics arouse more than your bile. Permit its ambered honey-arrows to unlock your skull, your breath, your dreams. Let its undulating valleys and succulent balm drown you in bliss-blossoms, even as its bloody courtyards echo with your long-ago cries. Do not let its excesses blind you to your own.

Undress your pride, and wander a while with these wandering words, without needing to know where you'll be staying for the night.

Everyone is selling something. Like an old junkie once said, we all push our habits. And we are all looking for release from the pain of our habits' grip on us—for we don't have our habits, but they have us—which just creates more pain. And addiction to release only deepens our addiction to the very pain or tension that makes such release "necessary". There's more pleasure in removing tight shoes than comfortable shoes.

Self-suppression and its compensatory addictions eat away our days. A very different, much deeper dance calls to us, but we're committed elsewhere, or so it seems. We may be at different stages, but we're all in the same boat, as close to the threat of shipwreck as we are to being unthreatened by fear, loss, and radical change. The more fearful we are of making waves, the more the waves make us. To make wise use of our time in the boat is to recognize that it is already full of holes, already sinking, already empty. The bad news is that in trying to plug all the holes we only plug up ourselves. Avoiding death deadens us.

Let us move more upstream now: Only one sperm ordinarily reaches and penetrates the egg, but all the others, at *essence*, live through that primordial and totally absorbing arrival, literally dying *into* Life, reaching the egg through their shared sperm-ness, unless of course they remain stuck in—or identified with—their apparent separateness and dreams of being a sperm who really makes it. And we are all sperm, at best swimming our heads off, and we're also the egg, the harbor of pure embrace, opening until there is only welcome, and we're also the matchmaker and the music and the dancefloor, the interactive space wherein it all occurs, and the power that makes it all possible. And more.

Though almost all sperm die before reaching the egg, at best living through the one or two that attain the goal, all of them matter, all are unique, all are individual and have the potential to be fully individual. And what is full or true individuality? It is not only unabashedly idiosyncratic, but also is in conscious, dynamic surrender to its Source, wholeheartedly participating in whatever contributes to its ripening, its transition from ego-centeredness to soul-centeredness.

Soul is the last frontier of individuality, existing as, but not only as, the self-illuminating interface between duality and nonduality. Soul is fearlessness incarnate. It doesn't mind death. In fact, many, many deaths constitute its ground. And many, many failures, failures that are *gratefully* taken as compost for awakening to What-Really-Matters. In short, Holy Shit.

The sacrifices required of us are overwhelming to whatever in us is less than soul-centered. "I" may claim to want Ultimate Freedom, God-Realization, etcetera, but no "I" really wants to be dethroned or made obsolete. Almost all of us would be terrified to not be centered by a particularized identity. So we constellate ourselves around the sensations associated with "I"-ness, rarely noticing that such "location" dislocates us from Being, corralling us in time.

Keeping exits open—confusing hypervigilance with genuine awareness—or keeping secret bank accounts—confusing being overinsured with taking care—keeps our awakening work halfhearted, partial, too low-risk, dulled by unnecessary safety nets. All the sperm die, all the waves end, but it's not the waste it may seem to be, if the sperm or waves live wholeheartedly, for through such fullness some intimacy with what does not die inevitably occurs.

Holy Shit.

It's enough to derail regret, not to mention one's train of thought. Acorns that don't become oaks uncomplainingly serve as fertilizer for the rare few that do become oaks. They don't attempt to destroy or discredit those that outgrow their acorn-ness, and nor do they idolize them. The oak towers above the acorn, but does not look down upon it. So too with humans who have awakened from all dreams. It is the slumbering humans who want to tower above other humans, without undergoing the necessary trials that are essential for such Awakening.

Making it wrong or disreputable or spiritually incorrect to be an acorn only needlessly complicates matters, given that just about all of us are still busy being acorns, brewing up quixotic mindstorms in a nutshell, dreaming of being other than ourselves. We as seeds struggle within our surrounding darkness, afraid to crack our seedcases beyond repair, mistrusting the green imperatives coiled deep within us.

We tend to keep our darkness in the shadows. We let ourselves be enlisted by our past, arming ourselves against what could truly liberate us. We become substrate for our dreams, inoculating ourselves against what disturbs our slumber. No matter how many channels we now have, it's still the same damned set, edited and packaged for more than our pleasure and less than our need. Comfortably impaled on false altars, we continue practising the art of distracting ourselves from our pain, the very pain that, if awarely entered, is our ticket to Freedom.

The dream's petals now birth "I"-dissolving viewfinders.

The ceiling and walls and floor now rocket far beyond the reach of thought. It's all edible in time. Eternity does nothing. So many rooms, so many dark and winding trails, so much sun and rain, all haunted by infinite possibility. Every story already dissolved in the Real. Recognition without a recognizer. Emptiness overflowing. Poetry outdancing meaning.

As everything falls away, everything is revealed. Familiarity is effortlessly consumed by Mystery, leaving us sufficiently decentralized to openly be, art least for a little while, the awakened essence of What-Really-Matters. No listener here, no note-taker, no author or authority, no sealed scribblings for future whatevers. No survivors. Just Existence, just Being, just the Is of is, utterly and unimaginably real.

Exactly now.

CHAPTER 16

Forgiveness: Sacred Closure

Forgiveness is the greatest weapon.
—Neem Karoli Baba

To err is human, to forgive divine.
—Alexander Pope

Forgiveness renews life by finishing unfinished business.
—Stephen Levine

Forgiveness is the heart's pardon. Sacred closure.

To forgive is not to excuse or condone, but rather to cease dehumanizing and excluding from our heart our offending other or others. When we forgive, we do not bypass nor gloss over injury, but instead embody a perspective in which injury is not given the power to obscure or diminish our compassion.

Although forgiveness might seem to some to be an act of acquiescence or weakness, it is actually an act of considerable power, for it not only retrieves us from the past—where we're psychologically and emotionally velcro'ed to those we won't forgive—but also from the future—where we're similarly bound—thereby bringing us present, undividedly and wholeheartedly present.

Forgiveness is a radical act of love not only for the offending other, but also for oneself. In forgiving someone, one is, in so many words, telling that person, "I no longer am interested or invested in having anything injurious happen to you. No longer am I going to turn the hurt you have done me into an excuse to condemn, dehumanize, retaliate against, or otherwise injure you. Although I may never again have or make contact with you, no longer will I keep you out of my heart, however difficult that might be."

Thus do we disconnect in order to connect at a deeper level.

We then stop feeding our resentment, realizing as we do so that it was actually feeding on *us*, consuming *our* energy and attention. Our appetite for vengeance naturally shrinks in the light of our forgiveness. Then the courtrooms of our mind are not so readily or automatically populated by us—wanting to be right no longer so easily recruits and centers us. We'll still get angry, but will be far less likely to infuse it with ill-will or hatred, or let it transmute into aggression. Caring for the other becomes much more important than getting even with him or her, regardless of the consequences that may be deemed fitting for whatever harm may have been done.

"Love your enemies." This may be the most *practical* (and marginalized) of all of the teachings of Jesus. Rooted as it is in our capacity to forgive, it cuts through the rigidly dualistic "I" versus "you" or "us" versus "them" mentality that so easily infects and aberrates us. Loving—not necessarily liking, but *loving*—our enemies is a kind of radical sanity, for in loving them, in wholeheartedly praying for their freedom from suffering, we are not only ceasing to demonize them, but are also aligning ourselves with their healing. Their healing—our healing. If our enemies were to find their innate happiness, if they were freed from their suffering, if they were to heal, then they would no longer be motivated or driven to harm us. Is there a more potent and user-friendly catalyst for disarmament than forgiveness?

Implicit in forgiveness is the willingness to put ourselves—and not just intellectually—in our offending others' shoes and skin, to the point where they are not "other," but only us in our less appealing facets.

Forgiveness does *not* depend upon what the offending other does.

That is, we don't have to wait for that person to make amends. (And, at the same time, it is essential to realize that we do not have to forgive until *we* are ready to do so—to forgive prematurely is of no more use than putting off the forgiveness of which we *are* capable.) Sometimes we may be so righteously caught up in waiting for and expecting our offending others to make amends or to say that they're sorry, that we don't notice we're being held hostage by our expectations of them.

If I won't forgive you until you "deserve" it, then I am simply punishing you (or seeking vengeance), keeping myself negatively *bound* to you, or to the storyline with which I associate you. If I won't forgive you until you have "earned" it, then I am keeping myself, however subtly, a victim of what you've done to me. And, if I am getting something out of staying in my "wounded" role, like a sense of identity or power or control, I'm likely going to continue to postpone forgiving you.

In the process of forgiving, we may well have to, at least some of the time, reframe the harm-doing we have suffered. Perhaps the pain inflicted on us by our offending others has, to a significant degree, actually been of genuine benefit to us; perhaps we needed to be hurt, disappointed, betrayed, left, and someone had to be up for the task; perhaps we needed to learn something that could not be learned without being treated as we were treated by our offending others. This, of course, does *not* mean that their actions should therefore be condoned or praised, but that they be viewed from a perspective that's *not* rooted in an eye-for-an-eye morality.

Then we can clearly recognize such harm-doing as part of *us*. What I condemn in you also exists in me (and in everyone else), and there's no way that it's going to be healed if I persist in treating it as something alien to me.

None of this is to say that forgiveness is an easy practice. For example, the path to forgiveness may initially be—and may *need* to be—paved with hatred. We may need to fully feel and express our hate for another before we can forgive that person (as is often the case with those who have suffered rape). This, however, doesn't mean that we have to literally act out such dark feeling with our offending other. If we can give that hate sufficiently free rein and voice in a safe environment—like that of good psychotherapy—we're not only going to feel, through our rage-releasing, a much needed sense of empowerment, but we're also bound to get to what underlies our hate, so that we can *fully* feel our hurt and thereby move through it.

And at the heart of that hurt—which we need to approach with great care and skill—is not more hurt, but a love that cannot help but forgive.

This love is self-radiant, naturally ego-transcending, at once innocent and wise. It forgives us our trespasses, our forgettings of the Sacred, our stupidities large and small, and it does so instantaneously. It does not make a problem out of our mistakes. In fact, when we allow ourselves to house—and ultimately be—such love, we do not see errors, but only incarnation's fleshdance in sacred transparency. Which is but the shortest of steps to remembering with our whole being What Matters Most.

Sometimes the process of forgiveness may seem to break our heart, but it is only the armoring around our heart that breaks. Or melts. Forgiveness brings us in out of the cold, potently reminding us of who we really are.

When we choose to forgive, we are entering the morality of the Holy. When we choose to forgive, we deepen our intimacy with the Beloved.

Forgiveness is the essence of activated kindness.

May we all embody it.

CHAPTER 17

Being Hooked Does Not Have to Hook Us

In the beginning…

First, we get hooked.

Then we get more hooked. Childhood passes; adolescence kicks in and overstays its welcome; adulthood becomes little more than prolonged adolescence, polluted by the habits of adulterated childhood.

We make excuses for being hooked, blaming our childhood, our latest relationship, government bungling, etcetera, for our hooked-ness. We get so hooked to our alibis that we may not even view them as alibis.

At various times we may consider getting unhooked, hooking ourselves to what we hope will unhook us, thereby leaving ourselves doubly hooked.

More and more, we arrange our lives around our hooked-ness, comforting ourselves with the belief that we're doing the best we can, even as we keep getting the feeling that we're missing out on something very, very important.

But eventually…

Having been somewhat aware that we're hooked, but not having not developed or deepened this awareness, we now begin to do so.

We lose interest in assuming the role of victim, despite the considerable rewards of doing so. Our perspective deepens. We begin to give ourselves permission to be in as much pain as we actually are. We sense that we are at a major crossroad.

We stop giving in to our aversion to asking for and receiving help. We don't let ourselves be held hostage by our shame over being hooked.

Then we turn, turn *toward* our hooked-ness, allowing ourselves to openly experience its underpinnings and roots, bit by bit, without getting lost in it and its storylines.

And when we do get lost in our hooked-ness and its dramatics, we extricate ourselves with far less fuss, not making a big deal out of getting off track or back on track.

As we stop making a problem out of our hooked-ness, liberating ourselves from the notion that to be free we must not be hooked, we start to really feel free. We become more interested in discovering where and how we are hooked, than in not being hooked.

Gradually, we develop compassion for our hooked-ness, and hooked-ness in general, without, however, letting it run the show. We don't reject our hooked-ness, being increasingly okay with not being okay.

Thus does being hooked cease to obscure Being.

And finally…

What matters is not our hooked-ness, but rather the kind of relationship with it that we choose to have.

Getting hooked comes with incarnation. It is not an error, not a glitch in the System. It helps keep us down-to-earth long enough to do the needed work.

Awakening unhooks us from being hooked on getting rid of our hooked-ness.

All of which is to say that being hooked does not necessarily have to hook us.

CHAPTER 18

The Anatomy of Desire

Desire can manifest in many ways, including biologically (as in hungering for food), emotionally (as in hungering to feel loved), cognitively (as in hungering for good fortune), and spiritually (as in hungering for intimacy with the Divine).

If a desire is particularly strong or compelling, we may feel as though it has us, owns us, runs us. Driven by greed, possessed by lust, eaten by envy, overcome with longing, consumed by ambition—all imply that we are at the mercy of desire. Thus does desire itself often get blamed for all kinds of slippages and screwups, as is most spectacularly illustrated by the kind of religious mentality that demonizes sexual desire.

We can, as is common in much of Eastern spiritual practice, treat desire as a hindrance, a trap, an obstacle to Awakening, thereby making a virtue out of desirelessness. Or we can, in typical Western fashion, indulge in desire, romanticizing "higher" desires (like hungering for marriage) and guilt-infusing "lower" ones (like hungering for pornography). So we can avoid desire or we can indulge it, or we can do something in between. But, as we shall see, there are other options.

To make a goal or virtue out of desirelessness, as occurs not only in much of Buddhist and Advaitan practice, but also in Christian asceticism, generates and legitimizes the desire to be without desire. The body, which is where desire is felt, then becomes an "it," a problematic something, an inanimate sheath or container—or housing project—for our "real" self, a disposable, chronically dysfunctional assembly of unpredictable and irresponsible meat, a mere animal to subjugate and tame.

However, we are not in a body. Our body is in us. Living not in, but *as* a body, but not only as a body, does not necessitate any negation of the body, nor of the desires that arise in the body. The body does not live on credit; its debts, including those incurred through spiritual ambitions, must be paid in full, or else we will be left to starve outside the Gates of Plenty.

Freedom from desire does not mean the cessation or extinguishing of desire, but rather Awakened intimacy with both desire and the sources of desire.

Go toward the root of desire. Trace it back to its origin, not to get rid of it, but to give it the necessary space and perspective to show up in the raw. Whether or not desire then disappears doesn't really matter. What matters is the kind of relationship with it that we cultivate.

Trying to get rid of desire is not just the ambition of spiritual fanatics and ascetics—just about all of us are trying to get rid of desire. Some of this is instinctually sane, as when we eat until we are no longer hungry, but some of it is just drivenness, desperation, the gearbox of addiction. For example, when we get greedy sexually—seeking happiness through erotic compulsiveness and frequency—we want to do it until our desire to do it is eliminated, voided, fucked away. Bop until you drop. Shop until you have to stop. Drink until you are numb. Splurge until you are purged. Lash out until you are empty. And so on. What is being sought here is *no* desire, the cessation of desire—the negative emptiness of satiation, the "peace" of oblivion.

It is not so easy to tolerate—let alone actually enjoy—for very long the bare sensations of desire, but we tend to like the feeling of release from such sensations so much that we crave having that desire, that compelling itch, again and again and again, so at to once again "need" release (especially pleasurable release) from it. This, however, is not deep release, but only a superficial discharging of energy.

Those experienced in meditation may noncognitively enquire into "who" is having the desire. This can be useful, but only significantly useful when we are already intimate with—which means getting close to—the mechanisms and psychoemotional circuitry of our desires.

Without the ground of genuine intimacy with the "less-than-spiritual" dimensions of ourselves, the sky that opens for us will only be the ceiling of our hungriest thought. We are not just here to live in and as Consciousness, Truth, Love, but also at the same time to live where Consciousness is attention, where Truth is paradox, where Love is attachment and—yes—desire.

At essence, desire is the primordial fuse and furthering force of Life, the bare condition and engine of being attracted, the sensation of every dimension of urgency.

Desire, in almost all cases, is desire for *something*. But desire for *something* will not truly serve our well-being unless it is allowed to be transparent to Being.

So where to begin? With our current *need*. With recognizing and embodying and directly feeling—including feeling *into*—such need, granting it full, unabashedly alive, and appropriately externalized expression. Breathe into it. Give it room to openly show itself. Don't allow it to detour into neediness (the desperation-infused, clingy overdramatization of need).

But what if we're uncomfortable with a particular desire? First of all, stop making a problem out of discomfort; get more comfortable with it. Then develop some intimacy with the you who'd rather not have that desire. The point here is not eradication, but compassion. Shaming ourselves for certain desires we have only drives those desires into an aberrating darkness, in the shadowlands of which addictions easily arise and thrive.

How reluctant we ordinarily are to simply admit outloud that we need love, and really mean it, not only informationally, but also through our tone, gestures, and timing. To authentically say "I need love" is not so easy—we may say it somewhat apologetically, passively, halfheartedly, flatly, suckily, or even defiantly, as if embarrassed or resentful to be so inconvenienced to have such need. But to be ashamed of our need—or to be ashamed of its intensity—is to be ashamed to be alive. Then we may withdraw from or condemn our need (or condemn its presence in others), or perhaps reduce it to mere neediness, with its cringing or seductive orientation toward its object.

We need to consciously and openly move through those times—as imprinted in body, mind, and psyche—when certain of our needs were first made wrong or deemed inappropriate or otherwise mishandled, times when we learned for reasons of pure survival to treat those needs of ours as pathogens.

Every type and every level of desire is worthy of our wakeful attention. Turning away from our "lower" desires only strands us from their hidden treasure, their dark pearl, leaving us in an eviscerated freedom, a spiritual wasteland of sterile attainment and disembodied encapsulation. Turning toward our "lower" desires does not necessarily mean submitting to them, but rather feeling our way to their core, knowing them from the deep inside.

Desire can bind. Desire can also liberate. It all depends upon what kind of relationship we develop with desire.

And with the root of desire.

CHAPTER 19

Freedom is the Final Nightmare

At first we feel so bad
Sure a fix must, must be had
Whatever takes away the pain
No matter how insane

All that matters is relief
Until we enter, enter the grief
Holding nothing, nothing but a lifeline
To what's beyond all the dying

Detox works us right to the bone
Until there's no minding being alone
Habits will not give up the ghost
Until we stop, stop playing host

Waking up is the final detox
Unraveling our deepest shocks
Dreams shattering in unbroken light
Revealing what is out of sight

On the way there are fixes to be had
And not always because we feel bad
When feeling good asks too much of us
Fixes remove us from all, all the fuss

Don't, don't ask so much of me
We may say when we get more free
Don't want, don't want that responsibility
Just want to play in the fields of mystery
Like a child with no tomorrows
Safe from the ten thousand sorrows

Freedom's the final nightmare
We're not really going anywhere
Here there's room for all

Sun and rain, rise and fall
What we long for is not so far
Come in, the door's already ajar

CHAPTER 20

Avoiding Death Is Killing Us

We die as we lived.
The chains we adopted remain with us
Unless shed while we were alive
After death, wandering through what we've made of ourselves
We are but a thought away
From the chance to leave it all behind
But death is not later
Death doesn't happen to Life
But is the shedding, the release inviting us
Into the Heartland of the Supreme
Beyond every possible dream

L ike birth, death is both departure and arrival.

At the end of exhaling, there usually is a pause, a gap, before inhalation begins. That gap may only last a second, but it is a second that contains Eternity. Death is much like that gap. On the surface, nothing seems to be happening; the breath is gone, the body motionless. But below the surface, there is plenty happening; dynamic openness, primordial presence, powered by the Breath behind the breath.

The secret of death is no further away than your next breath. Freefall into the gap between outbreath's end and inbreath's very beginning, and you will be cradled and filled by boundless space, effortlessly sentient space. Pure openness. The arrival of the inhale may distract you from this openness, but give it some attention as you observe the beginning, middle, and end of inhalation and exhalation, and you'll notice that this openness is already always with you. Just like death. As ordinary and mysterious as our breath.

Possibilities:
Death is a built-in breakout carrying reservations for
incarnation's transit lounges, ghostly stopovers haunted by craved
possibility—or launching pads into an awakening beyond
imagination.
Death is a compulsory loss of face and place, packed with
blueprints for another round,
another resurfacing of the same old bind, yet still just a dream
away from the Undying.
More possibilities:
Death is a mind-blowing tour of what we've made of ourselves,
followed by reruns directed by and starring those habits of ours
that possessed us until the body's end.
Death is a goodbye blooming with epiphanous hellos, but we
may be tuned in elsewhere, wrapped up in familiar clothes, busy
making binding connections with lesser greetings.

Death is a pregnant pause. It is the bottom line of in-between-ness. Death is not really annihilation, but rather just a dissolution of form, seeded with blueprints for further appearances, on every possible scale. Rebirth in darkly dramatic drag. Reappearance, not necessarily of us, but of Life-as-form. Inhale.

Death scares the shit out of ego-occupied us. No wonder we dress up corpses as if they were going to a party; no wonder spiritually ambitious "I" wants to be present at its own funeral; no wonder we go to absurd lengths to keep the almost-dead alive for as long as possible; no wonder we believe in an afterlife that's an eternal holiday for "I." It's quite understandable, given how scared we are of death. But are we reacting to death, or just to our idea of death?

We tend to keep death at mind's length, preferring a vicarious relationship with it, as exemplified by our common fascination with watching dangerous sports and so-called death-defying feats. Being so seemingly close to death may give us a feeling of being immune to or cheating death. Others succumb to it, but not us—a bit of comfort this is, much like sitting by the hearth's fire while a chill storm howls outside. But—exhale—the doors will soon swing open, and the night come rushing in. We are *always* close to death, very, very close.

We hear about near-death experiences, perhaps marveling at their mystical elements, forgetting that Life itself is a near-death experience. Right now.

> *Still more possibilities:*
> *Death is crowded with apparitions as real as you and me, ghosts that refuse to give up the ghost, phantoms of possibility recruited from our dreams.*
> *Death is an undoing of the mind-latticed personal knot, a brief outshining of ego, an unlacing, an unraveling, a mysterious yet enormously familiar traveling.*
> *Death is the arrow's release, a solitary flight into welcoming Light, or so we, nostalgic for the future, would like to believe.*
> *Death gives all the same opportunity. Death leaves no one out.*

Avoiding death deadens us. Getting intimate with death enlivens us.

This requires cutting through the mindset that views Life and death as opposites—- which is also the mindset that overseparates experiencer and experience, observer and observed, inside and outside, good and bad, and so on. Exhale.

Such dense dualism has as its operational center *me-centered* personal identity, around which orbit seemingly self-existing, discrete objects, things to which permanence or *constancy* may be attributed, but that actually are no more real than the egoity that grants them objective existence. Inhale. When objects—whether external or internal—appear to be definitively separated from us, we are dreaming. Exhale. But objects do not so convincingly stay "over there"—like objects are supposed to—when we start rubbing the sleep out of our "I's". Inhale with your entire body.

The more attached we are to object-constancy and to the security and kind of reality that it provides, the more fearful we will be of it changing, or, worse, being revealed as less than real. This attachment cannot be avoided—for it's as natural as it is inevitable—but it loses its grip on us as its objects are recognized as *already* being in process, as *already* being less solid or fixed than they appear, as *already* being not so apart from us, as *already* dying, seeded with their own end or transmutation. Exhale.

> *Life beyond the body*
> *Frees us to embody the Beyond*
> *Life beyond the mind*
> *Frees us to know the Unknown*
> *Life beyond death*
> *Frees us to die into the Undying*
> *Dying to live are we*
> *Reaching for What we never left*
> *But only dreamt we did*
> *The dream dies*
> *We don't*

Death does not slay us; denying or fearing it does. If we're so attached to our life that death appears to be a tragedy, a misfortune, a screwup in the System, then we need to bring more light to our attachment, so that its bittersweet nature amplifies, rather than sours, our appreciation of and gratitude for Life, as well as our compassion for all that must die.

About attachment: It doesn't deserve the bad press it gets from the pulpits of spiritual correctness. Attachment comes with Life. The point is not to get rid of it, but to keep it in perspective. Attachment makes painfully obvious what we need to face and deal with—insecurity, fearfulness, etcetera—and doesn't let us off the hook until we truly do so. Exhale. When we are deeply attached, our heart breaks more easily, but if we work well with that breaking—which is more a raw openness than an actual shattering—we will find a greater intimacy with Life. And with death.

Without death, there would be no growth. Yet we tend to fear death; some even claim that the fear of death is innate to us. But *which* us?

When we are *preoccupied* (literally so!) with being who we *think* we are (or who we think we should be), fear arises, especially the fear of whatever could threaten—or, in the case of death, apparently even *erase*—that particular identity. Would we be afraid, or as afraid, of death if we were to adopt a less antagonistic, less ego-governed stance toward change, a stance in which we practiced riding—and being openly present in the midst of—the waves of change, instead of barricading and consoling ourselves in sandcastles?

In crashes the surf, effortlessly leveling our monuments, carrying the essence of its depths in every drop, every surge, every lacy trace of evaporating foam. The broken wave, freed of its perimetering, knows the ocean, and in knowing the ocean knows that it *is* the ocean. And we are *all* coming to shore. Inhale. Thai meditation master Achaan Chaa says that when we understand that something (that is, whatever we take to be real, including our self) is *already broken*, then every moment with it can be precious. Exhale.

> *Rainy shore, shimmering sheets of darkly slumping sky*
> *Leaning am I into the windchilled thrill of daybreak*
> *Ocean thunder and a deeper thunder within and all around*
> *And I am ground, ground to sand*
> *Drowned, drowned in torrents of broken cloud*
> *Spilling shattered against another shore*
> *Letting the storm have my face*
> *Letting the waves take my place*
> *Letting depth unfold amidst stories too real to be told*
> *Letting go every should and every executioner's hood*
> *Making room for the sobering Joy to bloom*
> *And now my bodies are no longer just mine*
> *The body unbound, the body bright, the body dense*
> *The dreambody, the dailygrind body, the body doing time*
> *The body shattered, the body reborn, the body Divine*
> *Flesh of mud and stars*
> *Flesh of gravity, flesh of ecstasy, flesh of history*
> *Body after body, body within body*
> *All speaking their mind*

This I walk, letting the day undress me
Uprooted until I find a truer ground
Learning to surrender without collapsing
　To love without clinging
　　To be attached without shrinking
　　To know without thinking
　　　To break down without falling apart
To be lovers with both the Mortal and the Immortal
To die into the Real
Without forgetting the Undying One
Or the broken Many

The less intimate with death (or radical change) we are, the more shallow, stagnant, and unreal our life tends to be, and the more subservient we become to the very dualism that separates Life from death. But what actually exists *between* Life and death? Space? Time? No, because death, in the form of impermanence, is always with and within us, from breath to breath, ever *now*, already eating through whatever veils or gates we may have installed between Life and death. There is nothing more between Life and death than the notion that there is something between them. Exhale.

Life outlives us yet we are Life
Do not simply chew on this as mere metaphor
It is, and it's also something more
About which I'd surely speak
If my words were not already
Sea-gossamer dying on the waiting shore
And if I was not already consumed
By What Cannot Be Said
While I rock in the cradle
Of stories that cannot be told

Gradually, with great respect for our need to go at a pace that allows for sufficient integration, we shift from recognizing the raw Reality of what is to—however briefly or shallowly—actually recognizing ourselves *as* none other than That. Preparing for this includes getting intimate with what we most fear. Inhale. Entering the cave, feeling the breath of the dark. Exhale right down to our toes. Sooner or later, we let ourselves be unraveled by the Minotaur's bleeding howl of recognition. Its face, however bestial, deformed, or masked, is none other than ours. Inhale, exhale. Its dark dank labyrinth, reeking of corpses, is our birthing canal, the end of which we're dying to see. The end that is the beginning.

Here, where the nondual nature of the Real is unmistakably recognized, death is not a blackout, nor the Great White Hope, nor a metaphysical fable. Here, death is neither ascent nor descent, neither beginning nor ending, but rather a Mystery-affirming verb effortlessly erasing every metaphor that would try to explain or contain it, or reduce it to mythological fodder.

Here, the boundless vastitude and eloquent silence of pure awareness become more obvious. Things may still be buzzingly abloom, even heavily decibeled, but they're now playing out their scripts in a more peripheral fashion, no more disturbing "our" awareness than do clouds disturb the sky. Be still, be quiet: This advice from the greatest of sages (like Ramana Maharshi) is not about repression or forced quiet, but rather about allowing *intrinsic* awareness to become more obvious, more central. Yet even this is not immune to the self-aggrandizing of egoity. One must, at the right time, be willing to let go of particular practices; spiritual strategies, however sublime, can only carry one so far. At some point, one simply has to throw in the towel, not in submission but in surrender. Death, and a deeper death. Dying into the Deathless. Not to score brownie points with God, but simply because one is sufficiently ripe.

Death and Life together make and consume these lines, together giving shape and color and seasoning to Being.

> *All these words about death*
> *Now leapfrogging over each other*
> *In an already-exploded dream*
> *Is it any wonder*
>   *the Beloved wears every face?*

even that of the Lord of Death
Eyes behind our eyes
ever gazing into the Forever Wild
Homeland of all
Here
Absolutely Here

CHAPTER 21

Sloth and Torpor

It's really hot outside. Clear sky, no wind, neuroses out getting a tan. I'm staring out my window. Words come thick and slow, reluctantly surfacing, resisting my command to line up into some sort of topic. Sometimes having nothing in particular to say says all that is needed, whatever the fuck that means. Maybe I should just head for the beach, slalom through the browning flesh, and cool off, get up to my neck in the probably still cold waters. But that means driving down to the beach, 5 minutes or so away, but maybe 15 hot-oven minutes of trying to snare a parking spot. Funny how I have energy to complain, but not to get off my ass.

Even starting a new paragraph is labor. So why don't I shut up and quit? Writing usually comes easily to me. It'll be cooler tonight—I can write then. But the words keep coming, however sluggishly. Buddhist texts list among the hindrances to waking up the following duo: sloth and torpor. I'm guilty of both. They give laziness a nice ring. Have you ever watched a sloth move? My whiskers grow faster. And torpor—just the sound of it makes me want to have a nap. Who cares if it's only one in the afternoon, and I've only been up for two hours?

Sloth might be a bit better than torpor. Imagine *conscious* sloth—after all, moving very slowly can be very spiritual, can't it? Think of Buddhist meditators doing mindful walking, as if auditioning for The Living Dead. But conscious torpor? A contradiction in terms. The sunburnt blubber littering the local beach is about as alert as the fried jellyfish along the shore's edge. I'm slumping at my desk. Maybe I should do a bit of yoga, or even go to the gym. The thought makes me slump more.

Sloth and torpor—what a great name for a law firm, or a geriatric punk band.

I'm not going to pull myself out of my sluggish mood just so this essay can take a turn for the better, like a tedious film that finally manages to cough up a car chase. Is there anything more exhausting than enthusiasm pushing its agenda? I can see myself later on looking over these lazily wandering words and trying to extract something that is essay-worth. But I say to that unslumping wordsmith: Go fuck yourself. I don't even yell it. It's more like telling him to get his own beer. I'm not walking that far. I don't even have the juice to get the remote control in my hand. The couch will probably just stick to my skin. Maybe we need more support for complaining. I don't mean conscious complaining—that's too spiritual, too much work. Just everyday bitching, with all of existence being our uncomplaining ear.

Another paragraph, your unroyal laziness. I had a smoothie an hour and a half ago, and it's still hanging out in my stomach. Maybe I should just lie down. Or go drink some water. I'm always telling my kids to drink more water, and I'm sitting here feeling dry-throated, and won't get off my chair. Look at me sag as I write. The words come slower, reluctant little turds dreaming of making a big splash. I smile, but don't have the juice to laugh. I've never felt bad about sloths. If torpor was an animal, it would be a sloth on valium, the far shore of mellow.

I still have no feeling of where this is all going, so I'll let it go where it wants to, namely nowhere in particular. I could, of course, jump from this into some kind of reflection on ontological positioning, but I am thankfully not in the mood to do so. If you've stayed with me this far, you might as well stay for the ending. Have you ever been at a movie, found it boring or tedious, and stayed anyway, perhaps hoping that it would eventually get better, and then found yourself there at the movie's end, really irritated at yourself, wondering why you stayed through the whole damned thing? Welcome to the end. Don't sit around waiting for the credits. There aren't any.

CHAPTER 22

When Spiritual
Life Really Begins

When your honeymoon with spirituality ends—and it will end, marked by the arrival of STDs (spiritually-transmitted disappointments)—and when your affair with being spiritually correct and spiritually in-style runs dry, you may say so long to spirituality, but it is a premature goodbye.

Disillusionment with spirituality is inevitable and necessary, so that spirituality might be thoroughly deglamorized. When that disillusionment has had its say—cynicism's couch now being no more than a pain in the ass—and when your fear of reentering the spiritual no longer frightens or disturbs you, your spiritual life really begins.

Most of the books will be gone; the ones that remain will feel like old friends you don't tire of revisiting, even if only for a page or two every couple of months. Most of the practices will also be gone; the ones that remain will feel as natural to slip into as your favorite jeans or T-shirt, at ease with both being worn and being worn out. Most of your aspirations to be spiritual will also be gone; the few that remain will feel less like aspirations and more like unforced inhalations, okay in the beginning, okay in the middle, and okay with their ending.

The supposedly unspiritual will no longer be shunned. It will also no longer serve as a feeding trough for rebelliousness against spiritual shoulds. Guilt over wolfing down junk calories or trashy news will be replaced by a benevolent overseeing that does not make a problem out of such indulgences. When we are eating crap or reading shit, we will not make a big deal out of whether we are doing so mindfully or not.

Whatever disciplines we take on will result not from one aspect of us dominating the rest, but rather from a core recognition of what is needed. We may seem lazier than before, but we actually get far more done, because we are no longer fighting ourselves. Instead of being at war with our weaknesses, we bring them into our heart. Instead of trying to get rid of what we don't like about ourselves, we develop a better relationship to it. Intimacy becomes more our path than transcendence.

Seeking will become supplanted by living a deeper life. Questions will still arise, but will ask for something more real than answers. Alignment with the Real will become the ground rather than the goal. Details will cease being just details. Focusing on what might be will yield to focusing on what's here now; that is, hope will be replaced by faith.

You may seem more egoic, but your egoity will not be in your way as much; you won't mind its outfront-ness and characteristic excesses, anymore than you mind anything else that provides scenery and drama. Your longing to be fully awakened will still be present, minus the desperation and ambition that once characterized it; where once you were in a hurry to get it, now you are not rushing or pushing, having accepted the fact that you are in it for the long haul. Then, even when you are off track, you are on track.

Life after spirituality is the beginning of real spirituality. No fireworks, no applause, no pats on the back from the Important, no need to present oneself as someone spiritual. This is the beginning of true nobody-ness. It is not annihilation, but revelation. It is at once bare yet sentient openness, and also the beginning of true individuality. Everyday somebody-ness—self-centered individuality—gives way to nobody-ness, which, if taken good care of, makes room for authentic somebody-ness—or Being-centered individuality.

We go from surface to depth, then resurface, ready to be deeply superficial.

We go from flatlanding to ascending to descending to here-ing, realizing that though our self comes and goes, we don't. Life after spirituality appears to be a paradoxical affair. Somebody, nobody; nothing, everything; movement, stillness; these are only opposites to the mind. In reality they not only are inseparable, but also are not truly apart from that which is aware of them.

For every question that arises here, Silence is the answer. Put another way, everything supplies the answer. Nothing is explained, everything is revealed. Beyond knowledge, Wisdom; beyond paradox, Truth; beyond self, Being; beyond everything, everything. My words now start leapfrogging over each other, leaving meaning behind in a blur of laughter. If only I could translate the space between the words. If only I could say what cannot be said. More laughter.

Life after spirituality is committed apprenticeship to What-Really-Matters. All that happens is the practicum. Every situation offers the same fundamental opportunity. The teacher is everywhere. There is no freedom from our Freedom. No escape. The implications of this froth then still the mind, awaken and release the body, ground and expose the soul, unraveling all our dreams, breaking us open to what we were born to do and be.

And to this we bow, at once aware of and inseparable from our bowing. Such bowing signals our recognition, announces our participation, formalizes our awe. It honors the totality of what is happening. It gives shapeliness to our gratitude.

Life after spirituality is a constant dying. Emerging from our own ashes becomes no big deal, but just the way things are. We get up, brush ourselves off, and bite into what is next, bibless and happily anonymous, even if we are famous. Here the ten thousand sorrows and the ten thousand joys intermingle in unparalleled song, we their infinite notes, and we also the music that goes on, in the one moment that is all moments.

CHAPTER 23

The Childish, the Adolescent, the Liberal, & the Awakening

The childish take refuge below, the adolescent above, the liberal on all sides; the awakening take refuge not in position but in Being.

The childish excuse their parents; the adolescent blame their parents; the liberal parent their parents; the awakening understand their parents.

The childish sit under, the adolescent on, the liberal between; the awaking sit with.

The childish want someone else to be in charge; the adolescent want no one else to be in charge; the liberal are not sure who they want to be in charge; the awakening recognize and cooperate with what actually is in charge.

The childish confuse love with romance; the adolescent confuse love with freedom; the liberal confuse love with sympathy; the awakening are not confused about love.

The childish erect pedestals; the adolescent mount pedestals; the liberal level all pedestals save those of liberalism; the awakening need no pedestals.

The childish look up to; the adolescent look down upon; the liberal look horizontally; the awakening look inside their looking.

The childish are busy being nobody, the adolescent are busy being somebody, the liberal are busy being everybody; the awakening simply Are.

The childish indulge in self-blame, the adolescent in other-blame, the liberal in cultural blame; the awakening do not blame.

The childish turn shame into guilt; the adolescent turn shame into aggression; the liberal turn shame into impotence; the awakening turn shame into freedom.

The childish crave parenting; the adolescent fight parenting; the liberal legislate parenting; the awakening are self-parented.

The childish are at the mercy of others' opinions; the adolescent are at the mercy of their own opinions; the liberal make moral real estate out of honoring all opinions; the awakening don't take opinions (including their own) seriously.

The childish idolize the Sage; the adolescent discredit the Sage; the liberal avoid the Sage; the awakening make an opportunity out of the Sage.

The childish act helpless, the adolescent non-helpless, the liberal helpful; the awakening *are* help.

The childish swallow it, the adolescent reject it, the liberal trivialize it; the awakening respond to it until it's no longer an it.

The childish personify false innocence, the adolescent false maturity, the liberal false friendship; the awakening personify Being.

The childish open indiscriminately, the adolescent open suspiciously, the liberal open bureaucratically; the awakening open until there is only openness.

The childish fear hardness, the adolescent softness, the liberal solidity; the awakening don't make a problem out of fear.

The childish indulge in judging themselves; the adolescent indulge in judging others; the liberal indulge in judging conditions; the awakening don't indulge in judging.

The childish look after they leap; the adolescent look before they leap; the liberal look without leaping; the awakening look as they leap.

The childish assume someone else has It; the adolescent assume they have It; the liberal assume no one has It; the awakening are It.

CHAPTER 24

Greed Revisited

In our greed for the roses we are already wedded to the thorns.

In our greed to end or transcend greed, we don't recognize that in the very pulse of its desperation coils the pure and primal heart of our *real* need.

Excessive appetite is best approached not with the tyranny of repressive regimes, dietary and otherwise, nor with the permissiveness of myopic tolerance, but rather with a compassion capable of diving so deep into the dark of greed that it finds therein the pearl of bare need.

Shrinking from the thorns, burying them in numb flesh, or storing them in cognitive waste dumps not only strands us from their teachings, their messages, their pointers, but also exaggerates our craving for the roses. Trying to bypass pain simply tightens greed's grasp on us, partially because we're then not sufficiently present to truly face our greed.

Greed is all about having to have something so strongly that it has us, owns us, runs us. The repulsion that greed ultimately feels toward its object—and itself too—as it enters satiation often gets defused through the activation of guilt, wherein self-indulgence and self-castigation coexist in a stalemate that permits the "transgression" to continue. One hand grabs the goodies, while the other wields a parental whip. No discipline—just a knee-jerk punishment ensuring that guilt will continue. Greed has no conscience, other than guilt.

There's something grubby about greed, something dirty, swollen, redly suctorial. Orality in extremis. Just as fear has a certain smell, so does greed. Sweaty and dense. Greed stinks—and how could it not, when it is so full of shit? Of course, greed can also get all dressed up, including in spiritual robes, and it can also greedily gargle greed-disguising products, so that it appears respectable—a little driven perhaps, but what's so wrong with wanting to get ahead? When an entire culture makes a virtue out of greed, it's easy to confuse greed with need. We may talk, in a pseudo-spiritual context, of "having it all"—without noticing that we are then simply sacralizing our greed.

Still, there is a pressure to get rid of the more unattractive manifestations of greed, like addictiveness, and this drive toward "cleanliness"—polluted with puritanical, just-say-no zeal—rubs us the wrong way, inflaming our rebelliousness, healthy and otherwise, thereby just creating more garbage, more filth, more addiction, more desperation, more neurotic compartmentalization, and, of course, more guilt. Garbage—there's such an accelerating abundance of it, an outcast piecemeal archipelago munching away at the fringes of suburbia and our manufactured sanity, piling up and up, spilling out of our dreams—toilet bowls overflowing, sewers surfacing, plumbing malfunctioning—and poisoning our streams, squatting with increasing immensity in our headquarters, towering over the latest remedies for the mess we have made and are making. From tool-maker to garbage-maker—an epitaph already half-downloaded.

We waste that to which we won't cease clinging, if only by squeezing and sucking the vitality out of it. In our compulsion to hang on to and own what we love, we destroy it, crushing it in our well-meaning grip until it's just more garbage, however nostalgically or romantically framed. It is easy to get caught up in rearranging and redecorating our junkyard, diligently deodorizing or ignoring the mounting rot, instead of digging out its diamonds and letting the entire load of it be fertilizer for the roses, both outer and inner. Truly an unshitty thing to do with shit. And is not much of contemporary culture little more than compost waiting to be discovered, running from its worms?

Have what you have lightly, or else it will likely have you, and not so lightly. At the same time, however, don't make a problem out of attachment—getting attached to being nonattached is the dirty underwear of spiritual finery. Excessive distance from our appetites maroons us from their teachings. The prudish are not able to illuminate the must in lust because of their fear of getting in *that* close—the thorns just might prick them!

We may pride ourselves on not being prudish, but are not just about all of us spiritual prudes, shying away from our innate lust for the Divine, our hard-wired hunger for the Holy, our greed for the Supremely Edible?

There is nothing necessarily polite or neatly ordered about ecstasy, love, and real spirituality; there is nothing necessarily sexless or passionless about awakening from our psychospiritual slumber. Awakening thus is the greatest and the most consuming of passions, the most succulently engaging and nakedly alive—and nourishingly difficult—of passions, finding its optimal flowering in the unabashed presence of attachment, need, and intimacy. Full-blooded Awaring.

So dive in, for God's Sake. Through doing so you will soon enough know what to keep and what to release. The less the luggage, the easier the traveling. But easier said than done. We cannot truly let go of something unless we have already had it, *really* had it—or been *intimate* with it—in the first place. And to get thus intimate, we have to dive in, get involved, get messy, get attached, hooked, greedy, and all the rest of it—otherwise, we won't develop the needed *ripeness* for letting go. In short, we have to flesh it out before it can give up the ghost. Homesteading on the Edge.

Our task is not to create our destiny, but rather to allow it to *reveal* itself.

So dive in before paralysis again seizes the reins—better to have jumped in and gotten hurt than to have withered all safe and bleached and brittle in logjams of shore-hugging prevarication. We have a date with greed, both our own and our collective greed, and it's a date we'd do better to deliberately show up for than to skip or cancel. However repulsive our greed is to us, it is there to be known, and we cannot properly do so from a distance. Instead of recoiling from its touch, take it by the hand and introduce it to a different land, where Being is more central than having.

The estrangement from Being that characterizes contemporary culture breeds greed, its wannahaves and gottahaves giving consumption a bad name. Even the most pleasing satiation is not enough, being haunted by a craving for—and a subterranean doubting of—its repetition. Even the most sophisticated technological advances retreat before the loneliness moaning in the wake of their latest upgrades. Many religious rituals do little more than spoon out some release from the very distress they have helped create through, among other things, reducing God to the ultimate Peeping Tom. With such an abundance of dissatisfaction, is it any wonder that we are so hungry, so greedy, so fixated on "more" as our core mantra?

The good news is that dissatisfaction can catalyze a hunger for more than more. A hunger to discover the root of suffering and the root of true satisfaction. A quality quest. Dissatisfaction, however, far more commonly inspires not Awakening, but only a craving to be successfully distracted from our suffering, preferably as pleasurably as possible. So long as we adopt a problematic orientation to dissatisfaction, we remain seducible by whatever best reassures and entertains us—and such entertainment includes the horror stories of the news, the threatening implications of which increase our hunger for even greater doses of cultural and personal anesthesia.

The tremendous chaos of our era, with its crazily accelerating changes, avalanching stress, and time-obsessed social mycelia, provides extremely fecund conditions for cutting through the infectious case of mistaken identity of which dissatisfaction—the mother of greed—is an inevitable byproduct. This may be the Kali Yuga—the age of darkness—but it also is a time of unparalleled opportunity. It's all here all at once, not just metaphysically or archetypally, but literally—different traditions, different times and styles, almost all uprooted and thrown together in a dreamlike bazaar, a global supermarket between the vast walls of which ricochets the feeding frenzy of runaway consumerism, glazed with hope and sticky with greed, swinging between dilettantism and obsession. It's as if the whole planet is now just one gigantic garage sale, inviting us to shop until we drop, beneath the plastic skies of good buys.

But instead of just complaining about all the craziness—and such complaining is itself just more craziness—or glossing it over with terminally optimistic babblings, we can use it and its fertile chaos, its hybrid vitality, its bewildering turbulence, its underground hunger, as catalysts for Waking up, so that real sanity can take firm root. This means going without pacifiers and alibis, taking stands wherein crisis is not bombed, drugged, or jailed, but rather is taken as the opportunity it actually is.

We won't get any real satisfaction until we befriend our dissatisfaction.

How can we be fulfilled—filled full—when we are already stuffed, crammed, packed, filled up with what we take to be ourselves? Thank God for the thorns, as they prick the bubble of our gotta-have-it identity and its resident greed, leaving us in a position to truly appreciate the roses.

CHAPTER 25

A Man's Ego Sticks Out More

A man's ego generally sticks out more than a woman's.

Both can get in your face, both can go toe-to-toe with whatever offends them, both can take up a lot of room, but in most cases a woman's ego just does not stick out like a man's.

Thus protruding more, a man's ego is usually more of a front than is a woman's.

A woman's ego tends to be less cut off from the rest of her than is a man's.

The depth existing behind—a behind that is really a beyond—ego is generally more obscured in men than in women. In a woman, this depth typically gets more openly mixed in with personality, giving her self-expression more fullness, more richness and flow. This is why conversing with a woman is, for most women and plenty of men, preferable to conversing with a man.

A man's ego is usually more frail, because it is more cut off from depth, and so has to be more self-sustaining. This gives having independence an exaggerated importance.

Thus is a man's ego generally at once more exposed and more guarded.

The more it sticks out, the harder it gets, taking on protective coatings.

And the harder it gets, the more easily it does damage, and not just externally. This is where anger has stiffened into aggression, a much more common metamorphosis in men than in women.

None of this, however, is to extol women's egoity.

Men's or women's, ego is a mechanical "I"-making undertaking born to usurp the throne of self. It's just a habit that, unchecked, refers to itself as us. Even so, it needs not eradication, but right positioning and a corresponding transparency. It has its place and function, regardless of how it is demonized by spiritually ambitious programs. It's just that when egoity gets calcified, rigid, inflated, isolated from depth—as is more common in men than in women—it makes for a deluded and mediocre life.

In general, a woman's ego is in danger of being underdeveloped, a man's of being overdeveloped.

The fact that a man's ego tends to stick out more than a woman's has the advantage that it is more obvious, more easily tripped over, and therefore can be more readily given the thwack of clear seeing. A woman's ego may be harder work to fully get at, being more intertwined with her depths, and thus less easily flushed out into the open. At the same time, however, a man's ego is generally less receptive to such exposure, and so tends to remain more shielded.

The fact that a man's ego usually sticks out more than a woman's is not bad news. It's a given. What's not a given is whether or not we explore and cease identifying with our egoity.

The further out a man's ego sticks, the stickier it gets.

CHAPTER 26

The Practice of Awaring: An Exploration of Meditation

Meditation—the art and practice of deepening and stabilizing awareness—helps us to abide in and *as* Being, while increasing our ability to take care of the business of daily life. Nothing could be more practical than meditation.

Meditation simultaneously roots and wings us.

But meditation is not just one more activity for our egoity to master. We might think we are doing something which we label "meditation", but the odds are that what we actually are *doing* is just preparation for meditation. In fact, most of what is called meditation is just preparation for meditation.

The preparatory work takes effort. What follows takes little or no effort.

In the beginning, meditation is a practice of the self. Later, meditation is a practice that renders transparent the self. And still later, meditation is a practice that opens us until we are but openness itself, embodying what is *obviously* more real than the self.

That is, in the beginning, we meditate; later, we allow meditation; and still later, we are meditated. This makes sense not to the rational mind, but to that which cannot help but be aware *of* the rational mind.

Meditation undoes, unravels, renders ever more transparent, the very self that seeks and attempts to meditate. That self, that knot of subjectivity velcro'ed to spiritual ambition, views meditation as a remedy or as a means to an end, but meditation—if entered into with sufficient commitment—undresses and unseats that self, cutting through its reign of us, leaving in its wake what we've been all along.

When we allow ourselves to be centered not by our separative selfhood and its self-obsessed subjectivity, but rather by Being, meditation finds its true depth, the vast dimensionless presence of which unmasks, uproots, and ultimately dissolves our mistaken case of identity.

Meditation includes the overlapping practices of (1) making space—*transconceptual* space—for whatever arises; (2) remaining present; (3) witnessing whatever is arising, externally and internally, without dissociating from it; and (4) Awakening to the real nature of all that is.

Meditation is all of these and more, existing at essence as the practice-path of being centered not by self, but by innate awareness. Freedom from selfing.

Meditation is the practice of awaring.

As such, it makes equal room for happiness and unhappiness, simultaneously opening us to deep insight, the moment-to-moment feel of a soapy dish, and the subtle agendas hovering so very near to our next thought. Meditation makes conscious space—a true living room—for the high and the low, the gorgeous and the repulsive, the fascinating and the tedious, shining the heartlamp of intrinsic awareness equally on all, unseduced by preferences and weather.

Meditation is *not* about feeling a certain way, nor about being in a certain state, nor about having certain experiences, but rather is about remaining awake in the midst of *whatever* is happening.

Meditation requires no props, robes, or equipment. It is not limited to a particular format or posture; one can be still, one can be moving, one can be quiet, one can be chanting or praying or crying. Whatever works. It's good to stay with a practice that works for you, but not to stay with it too long.

And don't make meditative practice special or "above" the rest of your life. It's more useful to awaringly wash dishes than to sit on a meditation cushion trying to reach some exalted state. The good news is that meditation works; the bad news, at least for our egoity, is that the spiritual deepening central to meditation is not always going to make us feel good (see Chapters 2, 22, and 36).

Meditation is not about getting somewhere. In meditation, we move not from here to there, but from here to here—and from now to now—allowing ourselves to be Awakened and Homed by all things.

To be thus Awakened and Homed is to be grateful for all that has occurred so we can be where we are. Meditation devoid of gratitude is not really meditation, but only spiritualized avoidance and dissociation. Gratitude itself can be a deeply liberating meditative practice. As awaring and loving become more and more indistinguishable, we begin to truly live, regardless of our circumstances.

We don't *do* meditation, but without us there is no meditation. May we take the practice of awaring to heart, daring to let it immerse us in—and reveal to us—the full Truth of what we cannot help but be.

CHAPTER 27

Need & Addiction

Pursuing what we do not need distances us from what we do need.

The good news is that the consequences of such pursuit inevitably include enough pain and distressing feedback to remind us that we're off track. However, these reminders will insufficiently impact us to the degree to which we're committed to distracting ourselves from our suffering.

We often go to incredible measures to keep and house what we don't really need, while treating much of what we *do* need as trivial, untrustworthy, or something to postpone. In our haste and desperation to secure and keep on securing ourselves, we more often than not trample many of our needs, desensitizing ourselves to such an extent that we routinely abuse each other and our world.

And, regardless of how strong our dissatisfaction is, it may lack the power to awaken us, depending upon how thickly masked it is by hope, good intentions, and over-attachment to pleasure-possibilities.

In such conditions, our more uncomfortable symptoms become our enemy—ranging from "I"-sores to devilish adversaries—something to be erased or at least minimized, at almost any cost. At the same time, feel-good release becomes grossly overvalued and overprized, centering not only us, but also the airbrushed promises suggestively highlighting many a megamarketing campaign.

Such release, however, is little more than superficial relief, a pause that empties rather than refreshes, especially insofar as it dulls the edge of the very pain that we *need* to openly feel in order to begin reclaiming and regaining our true ground.

When we flee such pain and busy ourselves with a lesser pain, staying with it until relief *has to occur*, we put ourselves in a position where we so strongly crave such relief that we become addicted not only to it, but *also* to the very tension that precedes and *necessitates* it!

Thus do we fortify the trap, taking great pains to isolate ourselves from that pain which is really troubling us. And so our suffering suffers from neglect, instead of being recognized and used as a doorway—or fittingly personalized portal—into the very core of our needs.

If we didn't suffer from wanting what we don't need and having what we don't need, we'd likely never become dissatisfied enough to become sufficiently conscious—and appreciative—of what we really need.

Spurned, starved, or otherwise violated need is the primary seed and soil of addictive behavior.

Addiction is the compensatory and all but inevitable "solution" to survival-crazed need, marooned, orphaned, crushed, or suffocated need, need grown stunted or monstrous. Addiction asks for neither prohibition, as exemplified by the "just say no" bleatings of those with socially acceptable addictions, nor for permissiveness, but rather for the timely embodiment of a perspective that can both contain and transcend both "sides," in conjunction with an openly felt passage into the primal pain at addiction's core.

Do not look down upon the addict. We are all addicts.

Egoity is an addiction. Addicted are we to acting and re-acting, as if we actually are who we *think* we are. Addicted to a case of mistaken identity. It comes with the turf. In the spirit of the drug dealers we may claim to despise, we are inclined to hook our own innocence with our addictions, pushing—deliberately or not—our most gripping habits.

Furthermore, we tend to be addicted to being addicted, literally *occupying* ourselves with our most compellingly-appetited habits—the majority of which tend to refer to themselves as "I"—while rationalizing or even glorifying, such desperate wanting, such compulsion, as being genuine need. It's easy to confuse desperation with real passion or intensity, as if the fury, heat, and sheer drivenness of our *having* to have something somehow ennobles or legitimizes our mad search. (Many a movie has made such frenzy attractive, especially through eroticizing it.)

After the *honeymoon* of having has waned, you may notice that it, sudden pockmarks and all, now has *you*. Then you won't talk; it will. It will be in the driver's seat, and you'll go along for the ride, a velcro'ed ghost in the backseat or trunk—a ghost that won't give up the ghost, a muted child hammering against the inside of your chest.

But not all of us are addicted to having—some of us are addicted to not having. It's the ossified seesawing of neurotic accumulation and equally neurotic renunciation. In both cases, we are simply adopting a problematic orientation to our needs, whether through exploitation of them or flight from them. It's just the same old stalemated waltz of indulgence and repression, the crippled yes and the crippled no of misguided feeling. Nevertheless, our real needs still call out for us, calling us by our original name, calling for our undistracted love and attention, our unadulterated depths.

Need is to want as pain is to suffering. Just as suffering is the overdramatization of pain, want is the overdramatization of need. Wanting is tinged, however lightly, by greed. Wanting is fine, so long as it is not mistaken for need, nor permitted such free rein that it grows beyond itself into addictive behavior.

Need implies an object. Imagine need without an object. Does not the feeling of such need, however subtle, carry the Holy ache of mortality, the sublimely bittersweet burn of ripening surrender to the blunt facticity of impermanence? Again, imagine need without an object—is not the basic feeling of it dynamically yet effortlessly *present*, centering our every need for *something*?

Recognizing our needs for what they actually are reveals that there is no such thing as complete independence (or perfect separation). Individuality is all about coexistence with that upon which we are dependent, both personally and transpersonally, requiring for its maturation that we stop denying ourselves what we truly need. Genuine evolution requires wholehearted participation in the flowering of our individuality, including the needs central to that undertaking.

Like a ripe fruit, the fully mature ego drops—not disappears, but drops—of its own accord. If it is plucked before it has sufficiently ripened—as through the graspings of spiritual ambition—it will stay inwardly intact even as it outwardly decays, remaining indigestible, fit neither for consumption nor for compost, still clinging to its branch or vine, automatically priming itself for a return to its preplucked condition. Thus does egoity reseed, rebirth, and reassert itself, presenting its habits as needs.

We cannot force our ripening, but we can create and maintain conducive conditions for it. We don't have to rot on the vine.

Find out who—or *what*—it is that *needs*, so that you might become more intimate with the deepest need of all.

CHAPTER 28

Answering Suffering's "Why?"

When we are suffering, we may find ourselves asking: "Why?"

There is, however, no genuinely satisfying answer at the level at which our suffering is *the* prevailing reality for us. And nor are the metaphysical and "spiritual" rationales and beliefs spewed out by our intellect truly satisfying.

The understanding we seek is not in our mind. But it exists. It is first sensed when we cease turning away from the pain that centers our suffering. And it is found when we—in the form of awakened attentiveness—penetrate that pain so deeply that we connect, intimately, with its essence. Then suffering's "Why?" ceases being a conventional question, and simply becomes one more catalyst for opening the book of our life to the right pages.

Philosophically, we may rebut suffering's "Why?" with "Why not?" or with cosmic smooth talk. But when we move beyond these and other cognitive enterprises, our sense of identity shifts from everyday selfhood—which centers and animates the dramatization of pain we call suffering—to the selfhood that knows itself to be but Being making an appearance. Pain may still exist here, but not suffering.

So when you, in your suffering, ask "Why?", shift your attention—your undivided attention—to whatever it is that you are feeling. Thoughts may be campaigning for your attention, but shift, and keep shifting, your attention from thought to sensation. Don't try to silence your mind; simply let it be as you focus in on the feeling-dimension of your suffering. Enter it. Explore and illuminate its geography from within, touching all of it with care. See it without eyes, hear it without ears, know it without thinking. Don't stop short; enter it fully. Permit yourself intimacy with detail—detail of location, shape, texture, pressure, temperature, speed, color, directionality, imagery. Don't wait for a seemingly more auspicious moment; go, go this very moment, now. Enter it deeply, passing through it until you reach the place where pain is, in Ram Dass's words, fierce grace. Then observe who or *what* it is that is asking "Why?" Is it really you, or is it just a habit that has been given permission to refer to itself as you?

Check out the billboards lining your journey into and through the feelings that are central to your suffering. Notice which ones grab you, seduce you, hook you. Maybe ones like "Life's not fair" or "I don't deserve this" snare you. Don't, however, get focused on the dramatics at this point—it's enough to simply recognize that you're caught. All the places, faces, and embraces that hook us weave the net of our suffering.

Suffering can be one hell of a drag, but it also gives us an identity—I suffer, therefore I am. We tend to be reluctant to give up our suffering. What would we then talk about? What would we then blame for our failures? And who or *what* would we be if our suffering were to cease?

The end of suffering—which does not necessarily mean the end of pain—means, among other things, ceasing to adopt a problematic orientation to Life. Then every feeling, however dark or tight or dense, becomes a portal into Being, the open sky of which effortlessly renders transparent suffering's every "Why?". As Presence—the self-illuminating imprint of Being—becomes primary, and perception secondary, we find ourselves reassembled as effortlessly awakened openness, as at home with the ouch as with the aahhh!

The answer to suffering's "Why?" is not really an answer, but rather an openness ablaze with a recognition before which the mind gets so quiet, so dynamically empty, that the arising of a single thought is thunderously apparent. Instead of trying to get rid of suffering's

"Why?", treat it as a kind of divine appetizer, signaling a feast not so far away, to which one and all are invited. The main course includes the self that turns pain into suffering, cooked to perfection. Not exactly tenderloin, but quite edible, nevertheless, and easily digested when not allowed to become food for thought.

Suffering is but pain that's gone to mind. Instead of minding pain— thereby letting it fuel thinking and thinker—*be* with it, breathe it, feel it, inch closer and closer to it. The more intimate we are with our pain, the less we suffer. Ours not to reason why, ours but to come alive. Perhaps later on we will understand what is not ours to understand now, but that is not the point—what matters is the degree of intimacy we cultivate with our not-knowing. At best, suffering's "Why?" is like a roll of paper used to stir a fire; soon, it becomes food for the flames, its transformation its gift, the ever so brief calligraphy of its ashes eloquently traced across Big Sky.

CHAPTER 29

Taking Care of Our Opposition

It can be quite a test when we are confronted by the darker, more painful dimensions of those circumstances set in motion through our choices and actions. In the presence of such unpleasant conditions, we ordinarily tighten up, shrink, rigidify, withdraw, go numb, or otherwise diminish ourselves, ricocheting between defensiveness and submission, as though there's nothing else we can do.

Just as we tend to inflate ourselves through association with pleasant circumstances, we also tend to deflate ourselves through association with nastier circumstances, assuming the role of victim, through which our capacity for responsibility is abandoned for the shrinkwrapped righteousness of self-blaming or other-blaming. Thus do we pollute ourselves with blame's developmentally arrested morality and its supporting cast, in the melodramatics and ethical sewage of which guilt and vengefulness take turns masquerading as conscience.

Trying to make sure that we are safe from the unpleasant—as exemplified by insuring ourselves to death—only guarantees our keeping it and its worrisome ramifications in mind, where it contextually festers and reproduces with itself until it is *literally* fleshed-out, translated from the hotbed of its mental blueprinting into all-too-solid reality.

Awakening exposes—once our honeymoon with spirituality is over— what is not working in our lives, revealing key changes we need to make or at least open ourselves to making, but if we persist in obstructing, sabotaging, or faking such changes, we will very soon be realigned with our snore, dreaming that we are really living.

The good news is that as lost as we may be in our dreamland wanderings, oppositional forces inevitably will get in the face of the part of the dream that assumes it is us.

Opposition is inevitable *and* necessary, exposing flabbiness of spirit and every kind of complacency and mediocrity, generating situations that invite us, incite and enliven and challenge us, to Wake up, to hone and ground our alertness, to test and retest our ability to not be sucked in by our reactivity and mechanicalness.

As we begin to shed our blinders—or allow an increasing transparency—and to make the changes that we know we *must* make, all kinds of obstacles arise. Doubts may multiply, dread may colonize us, resistance may flatten or blitz us, family and friends may turn away from us. We may then understandably want to turn back, to exit the chrysalis in reverse, to numb and dumb ourselves down. Thus do the old ways pull at us. Familiarity is so seductive.

If we don't deal well with our difficulties, we may take up residence in disembodied rationality or metaphysical escapism, finding therein a consoling numbness. Or, more commonly, we may settle into a denser state of being, not leveling out until we have found a degree of opposition—or contractive force—that we can generally make good use of, rather than merely tolerate.

We don't get to move on until we are truly ready to do so, and that decisive shift arises not just from our mind and feeling self, but from our core of being, including within itself—and this cannot be overemphasized—the essential energies of whatever in us opposes it.

Before we can embody a deeper life, we must be able, more often than not, to remain grounded—that is, centered not by egoity, but by Being—not only in the presence of discomfort, unpleasantness, and opposition, but also in the presence of our reactivity and aversion to such challenges. This involves a skillful befriending and acceptance of insecurity, providing sufficient safety to let go of playing it so safe.

Being nonreactive requires the readily-activated ability and willingness to see and feel whatever opposes us as more than just something oppositional. This means ceasing to submit to—or feed with attention—our violent intentions and thoughts regarding our opposition.

Our work is to take care of our opposition. This asks that we stretch and expand and open, permitting ourselves vulnerability, a vulnerability that is a source of strength, especially the kind of strength that is utterly *unthreatened* by dependency.

Opposition is neither to be ignored nor bewailed. The point is to sensitize ourselves to our adversaries, without shrinking or thinking ourselves into their operational strata, so that we are neither stuck in recoil nor bound up in submission. Our work is to enter into empathy—however indirect its expression might be, or might have to be—with them, without necessarily locking horns and minds with them, until we can *genuinely* wish them well. Loving—not necessarily liking, but *loving*—our apparent enemies is a kind of radical sanity, for in loving them, we are not only ceasing to demonize them, but are also aligning ourselves with their healing. And their healing is none other than *our* healing.

So, yes, open to loving your enemies, but don't grovel or grow spineless in such love. Instead, stand tall in it, like great oaks asway in the push and slap of a violent storm, and stand soft as well, like grasses bending and bowing in the same stormwinds, losing none of their dignity in their prayer. Stand not like those who act as if they deserve the whip or insult, but like those who are alerted and further awakened—and are thus *healthily* appreciative of—the whip or insult, for only in so doing will you genuinely be able to love your enemies.

Our need is to know our opposition—both inner and outer—*intimately*, so that we might know *ourselves*. To stand in the midst of malignant contractedness or gross misunderstanding without abandoning or betraying ourselves is an art to be practiced with great patience and care. This goes far beyond facile notions of forgiveness, and far beyond merely trying to persuade ourselves that we are indeed transforming the negativity in our lives, for not only are softness, pliability, and receptivity essential, but also forcefulness, thrust, and bedrock-firm stands.

Having access to such qualities or responses is not so much a methodology as an ever-fresh art, through which we can touch the all without losing touch with the particular, finding a deepening intimacy with both favorable and unfavorable conditions, doing so not to reach What-Really-Matters, but rather to express and *live* It.

In taking care of our opposition, we take care of ourselves.

CHAPTER 30

The Masculine
& Feminine Poles of Anger

This essay is not about gender differences in anger, but rather concerns two primary modes of anger expression which, though labeled masculine and feminine, occur in varying combinations in both females and males. My emphasis is not on anger as a psychosocial phenomenon, but as an energy, a passion, a raw force.

Masculine anger is mainly a thrusting passion, feminine anger an enveloping passion. Masculine anger delivers lightning bolts, feminine anger an encircling conflagration. Where masculine anger is missile-like, feminine anger is a tidal wave, a centripetal avalanche. Both move toward, both speak through flame and fierceness, and both are equally intense and powerful, but they differ radically in style and shape. The goal may be the same, but the approach is not.

Where masculine anger is a phallic fire-bolt, feminine anger is an all-enclosing ring of fire, a lava lassoing. Shiva and Shakti. Step from the cosmic to the archetypal, and consider Zeus, armed with his thunderbolt, his huge and enormously potent electricity making the other gods tremble, with the notable exception of his wife Hera, whose less spectacular but nevertheless still riveting fury surrounds, closes in on, and consumes those who have dared cross her. Though she does not destroy Zeus, she is certainly not a passive spouse. The fact that Hera is not Zeus's equal is not a statement about his energy or power actually being greater than hers. but rather a reflection of the culture in which they were conceived and granted Olympian status. Shakti and

Shiva are purer models for the feminine and masculine poles of anger, since they are equals, their differences being more complementary than oppositional.

The imagery of anger in its masculine and feminine modes of expression is intertwined with the root imagery of sexuality, at least in its shapings and directionality. The metaphors of potent thrust and equally potent wrapping-around, so basic to erotic imagination, are central in the conception of anger in purely energetic terms—they may throb and pulsate less juicily when linguistically sheathed in anger's employ, but they are nonetheless still very much present. It is no accident that metaphors for anger and lust share plenty of common ground—both are anchored in an intensely arousing passion, the imperatives of which can easily bypass or override commands from "above" (one's headquarters), as when we are "consumed" by anger or lust.

If anger—at least in energetic terms—can be conceived of as a fieriness originating in the belly (locus of the third chakra), and lust as a fieriness originating in the genital region (locus of the second chakra), it is easy to see that too much focus on one (or domination by one) might outflame or override the natural intent or behavior of the other. For example, if the fiery energy in a man's third chakra gets out of control, is repressed, or is harnessed to an exaggerated appetite for retribution, he may find that his second chakra—his sex center—is doing the work of his third chakra—his power center—acting as a discharge valve for his anger, or, at the extreme, as a rape outlet. (Such a man literally is "fucking angry.")

Or excessive fire in the third chakra might take a different route, perhaps "rising to the occasion" and finding some translation and expression through inflammatory thoughts, which may in turn generate such stress, such tension, that the release possible through sexual discharge becomes exaggeratedly attractive. However, when our sexuality gets assigned—or *sentenced*—to stress-release and the obligation to make us feel better, we are only screwing ourselves—hence the unwittingly precise lament, "I got fucked!"

At its worst, masculine anger is a blind, steel-encased missile, headed by a poison-filled, indictment-clutching fist; all it wants to do is blast the other into subservience or even oblivion. It is a warhead too dense to hear any recall instructions from saner quarters—there is an enemy that must be obliterated, or at least punished. Such anger is obsessed with penetration, and, even more so, with unloading its bombs, whether coolly or hotheadedly. It has no heart.

And feminine anger, at its worst, is just as blind, being a recklessly unbounded, self-fueling wildfire, rooted in a desire to annihilate the other. Whatever obstructs it must be surrounded and gutted; its flaming pseudopods enloop offending material, then shrink the circle until that undesirable "other" is eaten by fire.

Such excesses, however, are not peculiarities of a few of us; we all carry them in us, if only in seed form. Their epicenter lies in toxic shame, toxic pride, toxic waste, for which no containers are completely leak-proof. What is needed—and it is far from easy—is a radical conversion. An alchemy that does not reject, but accepts and transmutes, and, yes, loves.

The fieriness and potent intensity at the heart of both feminine and masculine anger does not ask for smothering, spiritual rehabilitation, nor psychological marginalization, but rather for a mindful embrace that requires no dilution of passion, no lowering of the heat, no muting of the essential voice in the flames.

As I conclude this essay, thrust is present, but so too is an encompassing force, both working together, hard and soft, penetrating and surrounding, birthing through their encounter something that simultaneously is both, and yet is more. If such fire destroys, it is only in order to create. In its flames, resurrection is more than a myth. In its fiery heart, love burns brilliantly, ever replenished, illuminating more than we can imagine.

CHAPTER 31

What Is the Mind?

What is the mind?

We can list its contents—plans, comparisons, daydreams, images, memories, internal conversations, lists, judgments, and so on—but is there more to the mind than what occupies it? Does the mind differ from its contents, and if so, how?

Does the absence of thoughts mean the absence of mind? Thoughts and the process of thinking can be observed, but can the mind be observed when it is without content, and if so, what then is observed? How does the content-free mind differ from pure space? Or from consciousness?

When a thought arrives, where exactly does it arrive? We might answer that it arrives in the mind, but where exactly is the mind? Is it in the head or the body, is it around the head or the body, is it somewhere else, and if so, how do we know? And, for that matter, where is our sense of self? Where do we tend to locate it, and why? What is the relationship between our sense of self and our mind? What connects them?

When we identify with our sense of self, what happens to our mind? When we identify with our mind, what happens to our sense of self?

Consider the bare is-ness of a thought; hold it for a moment in attention's net, and examine it. Obviously, it has no mass, but does it have any color, texture, depth, or directional attributes, and if so, what brought this about? How real does it seem? Of what is it made? What, if anything, gives it meaning? And, aside from its content, what exactly is a thought?

If you are thinking about these questions, how do your thoughts about them differ from the thought or thoughts under examination?

Do thoughts really differ from one another, and if so, how? If one thought feels more upsetting than another, is it itself truly more upsetting, or has it just been injected or associated with an unpleasant emotional quality? That is, what exactly is a thought before it gets hooked up with other thoughts and emotional energies? Many thoughts may seem to arise in reaction to a feeling, but whether thoughts or feelings comes first, the nature of thought remains the same.

Remember that the presence of questions presupposes the existence of answers, and that the mind will supply answers even if it has to make them up. Such is its nature. Even so, there are questions that ask for something more real than answers. Keep this in mind, not as a concept, but as an awareness that infiltrates the mind, disguised as a thought, much like the awakening presence that may appear in our sleep-dreams.

When you are dreaming, how do you experience your mind? The body you have in your dreams is a dream-body, but is the mind you have in your dreams a dream-mind or is it the same as your waking-state mind?

Awakened attention does not allow the process of thinking to generate the illusion of a thinker, an indwelling entity that is somehow doing the thinking. If you think you are doing the thinking, think again, and take careful note of all the contents of your mind for fifteen minutes or so. You will very likely notice that a very high percentage of your thoughts and mental activity arises unbidden. You will also probably notice not only that it is far from easy to remain aware of all that passes through your mind, but that you cannot find a "thinker" behind it all. What *is* behind it all is not a self-enclosed somebody, but rather only what you really are and cannot stop being.

A thought held in lucid consciousness, a thought kept from developing associations with anything else, is a very fragile phenomenon. It is a kind of electronic apparition, usually not prone to giving up the ghost except when in the presence of awakened attention. A thought that arises in the absence of such awareness takes on substance through the attention that mechanically touches it, easily gathering emotional and physical support for its continuation, quickly spinning a web of associations in which we inevitably get entangled.

There is, however, nothing inherently problematic about thought. Thoughts are to awareness as clouds are to the sky. Just passing through. Are we the author of our thoughts? Mostly not. Have you ever entered a room in which radio, television, computer, and crisscrossing conversation are all on at the same time? Such is the usual condition of our mind. Noisy, self-important clutter, informational smog, packed with receptor sites for attention. Instead of paying attention to this, we tend to lose our attention in it, while conceiving of ourselves as possessing a freedom we do not.

The mind is the headquarters, the matrix, of subjectivity. It is theater of the abstract.

The mind is the self-organizing result of attention attaching itself to apparent objects. It also is the medium through which the offspring of this attachment—thought-forms and other mental phenomena—find relatively solid footing. The complex network of associations arising from this—a multidimensional mind-web—is what we commonly call reality.

But the mind is not so much the Real, as it is the Real's way of managing information. Thought-forms are primarily representational. They are *about* something, rather than that thing itself. However real they seem, they are but apparitions. Real apparitions.

The very tension between the mind's multitude of opposites and polarities—high and low, male and female, dark and light, young and old—provides the fuel that keeps it going. When the mind conceives of—not experiences, but conceives of—what exists beyond it, it runs into paradox at every turn. This is because it cannot, due to its very nature, actually directly apprehend what is on the other side of paradox. The capacity for this belongs not to the mind, but to the heart. There is a quality or depth of being that does not mind paradox at all, and in fact feels very at home with it. That depth *is* us.

The midnight pond is utterly calm, holding moonlight and darkness with equal ease. A thought arrives, is mindfully noted, and disappears into the pond, leaving no ripples. Another thought shows up, is not mindfully noted, and plops into the pond, generating ever-widening ripples, which very soon run into other thought-centered ripples, their crisscrossing creating patterns that, in conjunction with our sense of self, soon form the enveloping dramatics of everyday life. Even the tiniest thought, *if* unnoted, disturbs the pond, cutting us off from clarity and depth.

The mind is the medium through which we generate, store, and use representations of reality. Use for what? For language. For making meaning.

And for making a world constellated around our sense of being a somebody, a world that makes our somebody-ness seem real. If this sounds dreamlike, welcome to the mind-made complexity that is so easily taken to be reality, wherein objects sit neatly apart, as solid-seeming as billiard balls, bouncing off each other according to universal laws of mechanics.

The mind is the environment of thought-forms. It is a place with no location. It is a world unto itself, populated by habits that refer to themselves as us. To wake up from the mind is to be free of self-deception. That such awakening is far from common is a sobering reminder that we are more entrenched in and identified with our mind, and not just our thinking mind, than we think. When the mind is temporarily emptied of its contents, we might mistakenly assume that we are free, forgetting that the usual us is just a thought away.

Food for thought.

Keep this in more than mind.

CHAPTER 32

That Too Is Us

There's not much we have not thought—*thought*—of doing. It's all there, the good, the bad, and the ugly, morphing in and out of noticeability in the hermetic privacy of our own minds. The heavier or more bizarre stuff generally does its time in the less well-lit corners, feeding on backdoor hits of attention from us. We toss the beast—the smell and feel of which is never that far from our living quarters—a bit of meat, perhaps while simultaneously engaging in "higher" activities, such as keeping up appearances, or trying to be nonjudgmental or spiritual.

But what we are really up to is staying out of relationship—avoiding intimacy—with what we find despicable, lowly, or at least unattractive in ourselves. We might even rationalize this distancing as being essential to the meditative practice of witnessing or dispassionate observation, as if separating ourselves from our less-than-flattering inner workings is somehow a spiritual act.

So what do we do with our personal yuckiness and aberrations, our demons, our dirty denizens? Do we house them, do we relocate them, do we try to bury or murder or disguise them? Do we play vigilant zookeeper to them—letting them out to do our dirty work—or pharmacological trough, or literary agent? To what degree do we reject them? Sure, they are not *really* monsters, but only shadowed leanings driven crazy by neglect and misguided handling, but if we truly saw them like this, how could we justify continuing our violence toward them?

A favored housing project—at once an orphanage, holding tank, and trashbin—for our personal monsters is the conceptual dropzone called Hell, although it could be argued that cultures (and lifestyles) quite unlike ours provide for us an even more convenient dumping ground for what we can't stand about ourselves. In depositing so much of ourselves in those dirty foreign lands, in those ungodly religions, in those smutty back-alleys, and in that unseemly behavior of not-with-it others, we are literally all over the place, Humpty-Dumptied near and far. All the King's horses and all the King's men cannot put us together again, because the pieces—each waving its own flag—cannot by themselves see enough value in a reunion.

But the Real is not asking for a piece of you, but for *all* of you, not delivered as a forced coalition or a pabulum of shepherded submission, but rather as a true togetherness, a totality, a dynamic wholeness willingly enriched by its factional frictions and difficulties and strange mixes, along with the intimacy cultivated between them. The point is not to convert the broken many into the Undying One, but rather is to recognize them *as* that One, without any prerequisite denial, annihilation, or homogenization of their diversity.

Trying to pull it all together—especially when in the throes of spiritual ambition—more often than not reduces us to overgoverned mush, so caught up in looking out for insurrections from within and below, that we do not sufficiently realize that it all is *already* together, *already* coexisting, needing not some heroic unifying effort, but rather only an openness through which becoming remains peripheral to Being.

Seek God, and you won't find God, but only your dreams of God and what God can do for *you*, framed by hosannahs of hope. God comes more into focus when the difficult is turned toward and openly encountered, rather than just fled, drugged, lawyered, misread, or otherwise avoided. Limit God to what's above, and what's below will likely eat us from the inside out, injecting twisted bolts of passion into the cool of reasoned thought, spawning a toxic logic beneath the treads of which we get so flattened that we can barely breathe.

So let your make-believe self out, and the Holy in, letting what's between inside and outside give up the ghost. Let out every last pretender to the throne of Self, every last squatter and manufactured somebody, every wannabe "I", every last habit that insists on referring to itself as you—get them all out in the clear, not for obliteration or rehabilitation, but for exposure and illumination. Look at them milling around in the Holy's Courtyard, dressed in their resumés, all lost and all wearing your nametag, all veteran actors in your dreams, ready to play their part in whatever you are currently dramatizing. They may even continue to play their roles when you awaken in and from your dreams.

Why? Because psychospiritual awakening is not a getaway from dreamstuff, nor necessarily an annihilator of it. If some monstrosity or horror is pursuing you in a nightmare, to the point that your fear shocks you into realizing that you are dreaming, choose to remain in the dream instead of fleeing to the "waking" state, and turn around and face what's chasing you. Chances are that the feared whatever will change right before your dream-eyes into something more approachable or even vulnerable, but even if it doesn't, the encounter is worth having, if only for the experience of ceasing to flee what you fear.

Sometimes the Holy will intrude in our dreams—because that's where we mostly reside—inviting us to leave our slumber. But do not let your embrace of the Holy separate you from the subterranean, homely, dirty, and malodorous petallings of self—they too ache to be known and touched, to be deeply met, without being made the subjects of some self-serving salvation game. Stop making them sit in the backseat, stop pretending that they are not your relations, stop treating them like weeds, or else you will just keep Humpty-Dumptying yourself all over the place, dragging what's left of you to the nearest bar. But even in the dispirited downing of one more Soul on the Rocks, the Holy Wakeup Call still bubbles up, fluidly intact amidst all the frozen fizz and fuss, reminding us that this too is us.

The inherent inseparability of all that is is both the unraveler of every dream and the ever unbroken light out of which every dream is constructed. In our presumed separation from all in the dream that appears to not be us, we are threatened by even the suspected possibility of such inseparability, for the reality of it signals the nonexistence of us, at least insofar as we take ourselves to be.

But to consciously exist as the essence of that inseparability—what Joy! To consciously exist as Being—what Peace! To exist thus does not necessarily mean the end of our separate self-sense, but rather only the relocation of it, so that it no longer centers—and masquerades as—us. Being no more seeks to eradicate ego than does the sky seek to eradicate its clouds. In fact, it is only through allowing Being to center us that our individuality can fully flower—then every last petal matters, including those with which we would rather not be associated.

Everyone and everything in our dream is us. Every object in our dream is us. Even the space between the objects is us. What artistry! We lie asleep, while our dreaming mind creates a cast of characters and objects, plus a fitting stage for them, with us typically getting the lead role. Put another way, we identify with the "I" of the dream, acting out the relationships between that "I" and everything else in the dream. So when the scary pursues us, we take it to be not-us. Yet when we turn and face it, we often discover that it is us in dark disguise, and that it was chasing us only in order to make contact with us. Intimate contact. And light enters, effortlessly clearing the dream, leaving us as we are, present in—and as—what we never truly left, but only dreamt we did.

CHAPTER 33

The Upside of Down

Forsake not the lowlands of your days, or else you'll likely reach the peak half a human or less, crippled by your very ascent.

The most depressed of valleys, the vilest of marshes, the filthiest of gutters, await our awakened attention, asking not to be ostracized or transcended, nor to necessarily be transformed into "better" locales, but simply to be one more birthing place and burial ground for us, one more crucible for Awakening.

Holy shit.

Avoiding death is killing us.

Death clears space, makes room. Imagine if nothing ever died—a bacterium replicating itself every half hour would be a foursome in an hour, a clump of sixteen in two hours, a crowd of over a million in ten hours, and a six-foot deep layer covering the entire Earth in less time than you think.

But we're more than six feet deep in thought. Do thoughts die? They only seem to—they tend to exist even when they don't exist (like herpes viruses camping out under lipskin, poised for animation), ghostly blueprints needing only a shot of attention to march into our head. But thoughts—precipitated mind—crowd us only when we grant them solidity and emotional weight.

There's room for all. Death makes it possible and Love makes it inevitable.

We're the room and we're the all. Right now. Wanting to quickly move on to the next paragraph is no less significant than permitting digestion of this one.

Wherever we stand is Holy. Uneven or turbulent or murky ground carries its own unique teachings, inviting us to learn and embody a deeper, more flexible balancing, a more mature appreciation of hard knocks and immovable rocks and other troublesome whatevers. The quicksands of doubt need neither upsucking counterthoughts nor infusions of hope, but instead need to be seen, felt, intimately known from the inside, regardless of their resistance to alteration.

Only the weathered can truly appreciate climate.

Only the broken wave knows the ocean. Its shatteredness reveals its wholeness. Its suddenly wave-less "is-ness" is its identity, its unmappable and untranslatable identity. Its realization is not of understanding, but of Being.

If we condemn or flee anything in ourselves, it will multiply and fester and eventually occupy every exit, enlarging itself so as to seize our attention, encoding its outcast will throughout the apparently healthier regions of ourselves.

Shadows cannot be vaccinated against. Ugliness is just Beauty in drag. I remember walking along a road in southern India. It's raining, I'm barefoot, there's mud and shit and bright colors everywhere, toothpick calves and arms sublimely alive in the clear-eyed filth and blossoming day. Rarely have I felt so happy. Each step arises not in time, but in Being. I can't help but be grateful. Such grace. There's plenty of stench, but nothing stinks. My steps get even slower; since I'm going only from here to here, there's no hurry. Now there's only Beauty, embodied Divinity unveiled. Everything is pulsing to the same chant, lowlands and peaks alike. My mind is empty, my heart full, my entire being overwhelmingly alive with a recognition that renders everything Home.

A few minutes ago I was arguing with my woman over the phone, getting across not only what I was feeling, but also letting my mind put in its two cents' worth (to which it of course attributed a much higher value). In short, I was being a bit of an asshole, stopping myself from going into full-fledged asshole-ness. Not that it wasn't tempting. And so on. But unveil that ubiquitous drama—he said, she said, level upon level—and there's the same old Magnificence, the same old yet everfresh Beauty, shining bright, shining true. Now the argument no longer can successfully recruit my attention, and I cannot help but smile a little, feeling a kind of tenderness for my asshole-ness, along with a growing humor. This does not necessarily mean that all I said to her is now trivial or irrelevant, but rather that whatever in it that may be worth further consideration can now be articulated from a cleaner place. Sometimes the mud settles quickly, and sometimes it takes a while, but if we hold steady to Being, the mud will not take long to settle, settle down.

The depressed valley can be a cradle, the vile marsh a breeding ground, the filthy gutter a canal, the silly argument a springboard into depth. For some, dung is filth; for others, it is gold. What matters is not getting down about being down. "Down" is not "up" having a bad day. "Down" is where seeds grow, where roots fly free.

"Down" provides the ground for transformation. "Up" provides the sky. Both merge in Being, leaving only Beauty, only unmappable Openness.

Nothing But the Truth

Facts are not synonymous with Truth. Factuality—the actuality of facts—leaves out too much to be Truth. Facts can lie; Truth cannot.

However, though Truth cannot be reduced to mere facticity, and cannot be corralled nor framed, it is not elusive. It only seems to not be here when *we* are elsewhere.

To try to capture or preserve Truth is to mistake it for something else.

Truth cannot be stored in memory. Only the felt recollection of its presence can. Truth cannot be rehearsed.

Truth leaves no *direct* traces in temporal territory. The impressions that Truth *does* make occur in the Timeless. Wingprints in endless sky, the tracings of which can only be deciphered by undreaming eyes.

We cannot possess Truth, but we can let Truth possess us.

Truth is not just data, not just a reproducible headload of information, even though its expression may include all kinds of relevant particulars. However, to recall or go over such detailing without being present *as* Being is to bypass Truth—or be disconnected from its context. (To be present *as* Being does not mean that personality is shed or discarded, but rather that it is kept functionally peripheral to Being.)

Memory is not objective. Truth is.

Objectivity does not and cannot exist in the realm of the personal, even in the most pristine sanctuaries of scientific methodology. As we know from modern physics, the observer, however thoroughly sterilized or resolutely impersonal, *inevitably* has an effect on what is being observed. What *is* revealed in attempted objectivity is a deeply ingrown, depersonalized yet nonetheless self-obsessed *subjectivity* that tries to form "meaningful" associations with those aspects of itself that it can't or won't recognize as itself. This practice—engaged in by us much of the time—forces attention to focus on "what's-out-there" in a manner that seems to make a solid, self-contained entity out of the *apparent* observer.

The separation of observed and observer, regardless of its functional and aesthetic virtues, is simply an enormously entrancing fiction, an extremely convincing sleight of mind and perception that dissolves, or at least becomes transparent, in the felt Presence of Truth.

There is *no personal observer*—and therefore *no* controlling center of subjectivity—when Truth is fully present, but there *is* consciousness and feeling, there *is* sensing and observing, there *is* an intersubjective, naturally empathetic alertness. No one busy being aware, no realtor of information, just awareness awaring.

No one is objective. There is no such thing *personally*. Objectivity can be found, at least to some degree, in the transpersonal, not the conceptualized transpersonal, but the truly transpersonal. Truth's objectivity exists in its spontaneously positionless, self-less context, in the unbroken light of which which personal necessities and positionings cannot help but make themselves obvious. Optimal choices arise from an awareness that's free of its every would-be object, including itself.

At such times, the felt Presence of Truth becomes primary, and the perception of objects secondary. Then the Timeless takes up all the space, making room for all.

As Love is the Feeling of Being, Truth is the Perspective of Being.

Whatever happens to us in the Timeless is continuous with everything else that is happening in the Timeless. Memory is the scribe of Time. Truth takes no notes.

Remembrance of God occurs in the Timeless. Such remembrance is not memory, but always-fresh revelation—an epiphanously familiar unfamiliarity, through which it is all but impossible to take anything for granted.

In the absence of Truth, there is little more than fear and the efforting to be distracted from fear.

In the buttoned-up solidity of our days, there arise little fractures, cracks through which Truth shines, cracks that grow wider with our hunger for a deeper life, until there's enough of an opening for Truth to stand in our shoes and look through our eyes, through our hidden disguise, our reality-unlocking cries.

And what does Truth see when it looks through our eyes? Pure Being, Being in all Its extraordinary ordinariness, wearing every face, occupying every place, without doing anything at all.

CHAPTER 35

Trying to Be Someone Special

Who among us has not been seduced by the promises of being someone special?

There's nothing special about trying to be someone special. It comes with incarnation. However, if we put too much into it, we simply strand ourselves from our innate uniqueness.

If we work hard enough at being someone special, we become a legend in our own mind. Then, whether we stand out or shy away from the limelight, we invite potshots from our inner critics and backbenchers, thereby keeping ourselves conflicted and, ironically, driven to seek more of the "freedom" that being someone special promises.

Trying to be someone special may seem to be all about individuality, standing out from the crowd, and so on, but it is actually just flat-out conformity, mechanically acted out in the I-gotta-be-me malls of diseased desire.

The outer, or presenting layers, of our preoccupation with being-someone-special conform to the *appearance* of nonconformity, disguising the underlying pain which fuels our very craving to be someone special. LookingGoodIfItKillsMe.com.

In the mass conformity to false individuality—designer selfhood—that runs rampant throughout modern culture, much of our true individuality gets suppressed, ignored, misrepresented, or romanticized, its uprisings trampled beneath the well-meaning herdprints of our overfed craving to be someone special, someone really *worthy* of attention. The suffering driving this would, if openly felt, break our heart.

False individuality's personalized traits are differences that don't really make much of a difference. However much they might dominate self-characterization, they amount to little more than the presentation of superficial variations as *evidence* of individuality—different paint jobs, different set of wheels, different detailing, but still the same old deal, the same production-line vehicle, with the same mind-ridden phantom stuck behind the wheel, cloned from coast to style-driven coast, camouflaging its soul-numbing conformity with assembly-line nonconformity. TrulyOuch.com.

Disrobing our manufactured individuality does not leave us in a lookalike, thinkalike, be-alike mob, neither robbing us of idiosyncratic flair nor of the ability to take real stands, but rather carries us into and through the very hurt and alienation that has for so long *characterized* our lives and driven us to seek the designer traits of socially desirable somebody-ness.

This passage, this arduous and immeasurably rewarding descent, transports us both into our common Unity of Being *and* into the fleshing-out and ripening of our own innate uniqueness.

This is not about trying to be nobody special (there's not a much more advanced case of spiritual conceit than that of making a holy grail out of nobody-ness). The key is not to negate selfhood, nor to worship or indulge it, but to permit it such rich transparency relative to Being, that it cannot help but colorfully represent and reveal us. Doing so is an uncopyable art, rather than just another self-improvement program, asking that we see through and let go of our trying to be somebody, nobody, anybody special.

To this end, we need to pay more attention to our craving for attention. Looking to be made visible by attention—both ours and others—is, among other things, an effort to prove not only that we matter, but that *we exist*.

When we are truly ourselves, our attention—and that of others—cannot significantly corrupt, divert, or sedate us. At such times, our attention becomes wider, deeper, more awakened, sometimes becoming conscious of itself and its source, so that the noticing of particulars coexists with—and even becomes functionally secondary—to the bare awareness of Being.

Those caught up in false individuality—trying to be *somebody* special—do not know how to surrender, being mired in neurotic independence. Those caught up in false togetherness—trying to be *nobody* special—do not know how to take a real stand, being mired in neurotic dependence. Neither knows intimacy. Both are scrambling for position in a no-one's-land, all wrapped up in their flags, growing weapons in each other's shadow.

Our essential somebody-ness is our unique piece to play and honor, already perfectly fit for a necessarily sacrificial process in which innumerable self-conscious appearances flirt with eternal anonymity, trying to know themselves without knowing the others, in a Cosmos pervaded by both multisensory deception and a sublime knowingness that the mind cannot tap nor imagine.

To offset its inevitable separation-anxiety, false individuality is chronically on the hunt for ways to feel better, not recognizing that what it is *really* seeking release from is *itself.*

Die into a deeper individuality, an individuality expressive of your innate uniqueness, providing no seats for your increasingly vestigial audience, no tickets, no solidity, no promise of spiritual kudos. Make the necessary effort, so that you might become more intimate with the necessary non-effort. Fully develop and flesh out your uniqueness, keeping it mindful of its mortality, letting it be an offering to That Which birthed it.

To do so is the essence of being human. Freedom in the flesh.

CHAPTER 36

Getting Spiritual

If we actually knew what we were getting into when we first talked ourselves into entering spirituality's domain, we likely would turn the other way. The notion of getting spiritual has to look good to us, has to pack plenty of promise; it has to be infused with an appeal that seriously hooks us, that takes major advantage of our dissatisfaction.

So feeling good is the initial bait. Feeling even better is the bait once we're through the door. Drinks may be on the house, at least for the first round or two. Then, when it's far from easy to go back, the game takes a turn we didn't expect. The shiny new thing we just bought starts breaking down. Difficulties surface. Neuroses gatecrash our equanimity. Groundlessness greets our step. Just a test of faith, we may tell—or are told to tell—ourselves, but such self-talk is not the kind of company we were expecting. The oasis seems to be slipping away, now more shady than green, leaving us dry and not-so-high. And no money-back policies. Holy shit.

And because the payoff usually does not yield feel-good results all that quickly—or at least as quickly as sex—the promises have to be Big. Dangling before us in horizon-expanding capitals are Freedom, Enlightenment, and Happiness. We may be told that getting spiritual is more blissful than anything else. All that's needed is an open mind— and open wallet, some might add. Come in, blare billboards behind our forehead, the banquet is ready, all laid out for you, asking for just a few minutes of your time. Bite in, get your teeth into it, forget about bibs, party on, spiritual you!

So in we go, greedy as Boxing Day shoppers. And why not? Why not be all we can be? Why not be a wiser, kinder, brighter, more spiritual us? Who can argue against this? A cautious place in us may recommend reading the fine print, but we may be so sick of holding back, being halfhearted, eating leftovers, trudging through our days, and so on, that we say the hell with it, let's go! Even permitting such an attitude feels good, appropriately rebellious, so we loosen our ties and belts, unbutton our appetite, march through the gates.

Buying into sunny-side up spirituality, however, leaves us with little more than egg on our face and a big bill.

But let's not be unkind here. We have to start somewhere. Learning is an inherently messy process. Even the tackiest of spiritual malls offer something of value, if only by turning us toward better quality. We don't, at least initially, need to hear all about the upcoming trials of the soul, anymore than a just-pregnant-for-the-first-time woman needs to hear all about how painful childbirth is probably going to be. We already, in our depths, can sense the difficulties and challenges that will be coming, but don't need to prematurely focus on them. We don't need to know how many times we will have to fall before we can truly stand.

At the same time, however, we can only afford to spend so much time in spirituality's playpens. If we wait too long to take out our pacifiers, we may get so stuck in having to be comfortable that we don't really live, but just get by, reducing our spirituality to a conceptual oasis under the plastic palms of which we do our time.

Do we really need to read yet another book informing us that we are all One, or that every cloud has a silver lining, or that all we have to do is love each other? However well-intentioned such offerings might be, they generally just add to the information smog in which we are already suffocating. Whether the lemmings think they are all one or not as they go over the cliff matters little.

Spiritual teachings that strike home may state already-familiar principles, but do so in an original manner. An obviously unique rendering of a teaching has more awakening power than a parroting of it. A fresh, creative voicing tends to catalyze more vitality, more spark, more interest, more bare appreciation—the bloom is still the bloom, but its aroma, texture, color, beauty and basic being can be more fully taken in when creatively presented, because we are then more fully engaged, connected in more places, plugged in at more sites.

When we have assimilated a teaching, we don't have to present it the same way every time we share it. We can transmit it differently for each person, and each occasion. Truth cannot be rehearsed. To present what we have learned in a vital and creative manner asks that we stay ever-fresh and open to it, as if feeling and knowing it for the first time. It is that fresh delivery that impacts the recipient. The wilted lettuce of cut-and-dried learnings does not nourish. If we are told that it should nourish us, and we tell ourselves the same thing—pretending that it is not wilted—then we're not likely going to get much out of taking it in. At best, it'll be food for thought.

How many more regurgitated teachings can you hear without reaching for the candy or remote control or whatever else has been designated spiritually incorrect? How much more spiritual pabulum can you endure before you fry up a bloody steak or read a bunch of trashy news? We tend to go where the juice is, and if we have waited too long, we will not be particularly discriminating as to where we go to be with what's crisp or succulent.

Go for what is fresh. Not necessarily new, but fresh. The Buddha's bottom-line sutras are over 2500 years old, but are absolutely fresh coming from firsthand experience of them. If it's not fresh, why try to make a meal out of it? Why make a spiritual virtue out of feeding on leftovers? Fresh may not always feel good—for sometimes it has to be bitter, for both awakening and digestive purposes—but it serves us. Stale lacks energy; stale sucks our energy; stale feeds on us.

Don't be food for lifeless or secondhand teachings. Use your teeth. When you bite into what is before you, the freshness of it, the juiciness and vitality of it, will immediately be evident. To thus bite is not just to mechanically chomp into what's upon your plate, but to penetrate below its surface so as to get a direct feel for its core qualities. Nice people don't bite deep. Instead of being nice, be real. Bite in. Release and contact the vital energies of whatever is before you, realizing that it's all food.

Now this essay is trying to boomerang its way back to its beginning, wondering how the hell it got from there to here. But maybe it does not need to be neatly tied together. Spirituality is the ultimate feast. It looks so yummy at first, such a gorgeous tableful of wonders. Eventually we realize that we are part of the feast, and things don't look so yummy. One gigantic sacrifice. At last we stop worrying about what happens when everything gets eaten, because the feast does not end. Its dishes come and go, as do our experiences and myriad selves, but we don't.

CHAPTER 37

How Old Are You?

Wisdom does not necessarily come with age, but age makes possible a wisdom not otherwise available, if we will but open to it.

Age viewed with ageless eyes is but ripened Beauty. Old wine, sunset-stained leaves, a near-century of laugh lines. Only the weathered can truly appreciate climate.

But we still tend to marginalize the elderly, for they remind us of what we will all too soon become. We admire those who don't look their age—although we sometimes might like them to act their age—perhaps envying them their relative youth, while forgetting that they are decaying just the slightest bit slower than us.

If we won't embrace our aging, we will likely not feel particularly welcoming of Death when it comes. It's fine to invest energy into keeping our body in good health, but to get overattached to it remaining in good health only wears us out. Being able to do backbends at 75 is less important than being psychospiritually flexible at 75. Suppleness of body has its season; suppleness of mind knows no seasons; suppleness of spirit has room for it all.

There are now more "elderly" professional athletes than ever before. When one athlete ran a sub four-minute mile at the age of 41, I was very impressed, and for a short while fantasized about lowering my running times. A few hard training sessions took the legs out of my enthusiasm, but my fascination persisted for a while. Even now, I still sometimes find myself childishly proud of how well I'm doing physically.

Being intimate with agelessness allows us to age well. My body may be 56, my mind may be grooved with 56 years of patterning, but how old really am I? Can I really be absolutely sure of when I began? Can I be absolutely sure there even was a beginning? Living as a mind may mean being stuck in time, and living as a body may mean being stuck in space, but living as what I actually am naturally transcends time, and therefore also space, leaving me—as I truly am—with no fixed location, no temporal-spatial coordinates, and thus nowhere to go, even as I make and keep appointment times.

My lower back hurts this morning. It hasn't hurt for years. I see my head in profile while I'm buying a new jacket, and am a bit surprised— am I really *that* bald? And look at those lines—it must be the lighting, or maybe the lousy sleep I had last night. And so on. Vanity does not die easily. The *Abidharma*, the source writings of ancient Buddhist psychology, says that conceit is one of the last hindrances to go, persisting until just before Nirvanic realization takes root.

Aging can, however, lessen the grip the comparing mind has on us, allowing us to sit back more, to rest on easygoing verandahs while those younger than us go about their business, all but oblivious to our increasingly compassionate eye. We watch sandcastles going up and up, cemented with pride and dreams of glory; we watch the tide rolling in, effortlessly crumbing every last castle; we hear the upset and fuss over this; and we don't lose our equanimity.

We don't have to be toothless and half-senile to be capable of this; all that is needed is a nonproblematic orientation to our aging. The yells of exultation and the yells of upset expectations both blend and disappear in the soothing roar of the waves, and we feel through all the dying a kinship with all that is. One moment we are taking our first step, and the next we are balancing on eighty-year old arthritic legs.

The clouds vanish, but the sky remains. Aging makes this profoundly obvious, if we will but look through ageless eyes.

Such an art it, to let our aging mature us.

CHAPTER 38

Teasing Trips Us
Up On Our Way Down

Teasing is an art.

Sometimes its palette is crude, its routine and transitions rough or rude, its delivery little more than a heavy-handed coloring outside the lines, but still it is trying to say something without saying it literally or flatly.

Other times, teasing is more tuned-in, as when it breaks up emotional logjams-in-waiting by adroitly disrobing and jousting with foibles and sore points. Teasing then gets in our face in a way that allows us to more easily lose face; our self-importance and its neurotic sidekicks find a quick and relatively painless deflation in the artful presence of teasing's pointed humor. Teasing can be the short way home.

Relationships devoid of teasing easily flatline into deadening associations. Maneuvering around the eggshells of psychospiritually correct, let's-not-offend-anyone relationship doesn't make for much intimacy. A frozen dance of wallflowers. Teasing can get us back out onto a dancefloor where there is plenty of room for passion and color and multileveled movement. Toes may get stepped on, extravagant flourishes may occur, but there is no doubt that aliveness is afoot.

At the same time, teasing, if it has heart, doesn't overplay its hand or force us to move, and nor does it shame us, though it may bring us more into touch with the shame we already carry. Through its penetrating angles and creative turns, teasing can provide channels through which our previously held-in shame can flow and dissipate.

Tuned-in teasing pulls down the pants of our neurotic rituals before an incisive yet compassionate eye, putting down our sweaty fretting and fussing without putting us down. An incisive yet affectionate lampooning this is, surfing the edge of discomfort while providing enough good humor to give that edge more roundedness, more softness. Teasing can be very cost-effective therapy. It is impromptu psychodrama.

Skillful teasing provides a dramatization that deflates our self-possessed dramatics.

Its wit and exaggerations of delivery create an instant stage, under the lights of which our habits mill about like dazed cattle waiting to be branded. Here a moo, there a moo, no longer masquerading as a you, unzipped by teasing's touch, leaving not more drama, nor more bovinity, but only refreshed us, only liberated energy.

Good teasing finds the edge, sets up camp there, takes in the view, and delivers, finding a vital, sparky balance in its precarious positioning. The ledge may cave in, the tent blow away, the weather suddenly change, but teasing then finds fresh ground, if only for a moment. Its lack of solid footing only sharpens its focus.

Teasing is conversational catharsis, using laughter in the same way that awareness of deep loss uses crying. It can bananapeel our overdone concerns, with invisible clowns lining both sides of our spill. Teasing can lighten our load.

Teasing trips us up on our way down. As much as it may flabbergast, shock, irritate, annoy, discombobulate, or insult us, tuned-in teasing invites us to realign ourselves with what-really-matters.

Teasing is a simultaneous testing and tasting of uncertain or potentially turbulent waters. It may nudge us toward deeper waters, but it does not shove us. It may broadly hint of bigger steps or risks, but it does not demand them. In its edgy yet friendly presence, we may find unexpected room to consider things we wouldn't have otherwise considered. We might even get to rehearse some new steps, without the usual critical eye having so much power to hobble us.

Teasing's intent matters as much as its delivery. If we do not have the well-being of the other as a priority, then we'd do better not to launch ourselves into teasing that person. If, for example, I am angry at you, and I start teasing you, I may find myself crossing the line into sarcasm and even contempt, while telling you that I am just joking when you express your hurt at what I am saying. We don't tease to score points, although we might blow the whistle on our desire to do so, right in the midst of teasing, which only adds to the life-giving energy of our teasing.

Teasing lets us sniff out uncomfortable edges with more-than-usual looseness. It scouts ahead for signs, absorbing data—reactions, movements, attitudes—so quickly that its next sentence may well be modified on-the-spot to better suit the terrain just around the next corner. In teasing's instant dramatics, we simultaneously are our roles and are not our roles; all we need do is plunge in, scriptlessly alert, ready, curious.

Well-delivered teasing tests the health and resiliency of our edges, keeping us fluid, even if our bones are brittle with age. It is the leavening of healthy criticism. It is raw theater, psychologically astute theater, theater of the practical absurd, with funny-bone scaffolding, wonderfully irritating savvy, and annoyingly awakening scene shifts, ever turning shit to wit.

CHAPTER 39

On the Art of
Being Deeply Superficial

Aparticipant in a group once unhappily and very earnestly told me he wanted to "go deeper." It was obvious that he was torturing himself with spiritual expectation—he'd just returned from India, he somberly announced, as he sat waiting for me to help him "go deeper."

My immediate response was: "You need to be superficial."

He brightened a little, suddenly boyish, his puzzlement rapidly unwrinkling. I told him he was trying so hard to be spiritual, to be deep, to be a somebody who was really going for it, that he'd made a problem out of the superficial, as if the waves were somehow less significant or relevant than the currents deep below them.

As his forehead started to wrinkle up again, I said, "You need to be *profoundly* superficial!"

When we truly "go deep," there is no inner evaluator telling us that, yes, we have done so. No awards, no applause, no cosmic pat on the back, no self to claim spiritual attainment. At such times, the separation between surface and depth is far from concrete, perhaps even ceasing to exist, and we recognize that Being-ness is just as present in—and as—the superficial as the deep.

Profoundly superficial. Try it. Give it a go. Dive into it, without letting it become the latest carrot for spiritualized egoity's quest for self-transcendence. Being profoundly superficial doesn't mean being stuck in shallowness, and nor does it mean residing in enforced lightheartedness. It doesn't actually mean anything, existing as simply an invitation to skinny-dip in the Unimaginable Unknown. The moonlight laying shattered upon the sea has no depth yet displays fathomless shades of blazing deep.

It's all bottomless.

The shift required of us is not even a movement, though it may secondarily involve considerable movement. Let the seeker in you dissolve—or return to its elemental origins—and you'll discover that Being is already the case, already here, already appearing as you, including the most utterly superficial and stubbornly fixated you.

Remember how preschoolers play. Surface and depth having a ball together. It's as if no one is watching. No splitting of self. No rehearsal. Just pure dance, minus wallflowers and judges. We may think we have outgrown such play, but in fact we have mostly only adult-erated it.

So let us open to our superficiality, let us not exclude play from our spiritual practice, let us be light-footed in our deepness, remaining intimate with the kind of wonder that leaves our minds speechless. If we avoid such openness, we'll likely remain chained to the familiar, reducing the Holy Deep to an object, a something we can think about and get busy seeking.

But the depth we seek is right here, even if we are trying to convince ourselves otherwise. Every moment is the Big Moment. What happens after Death is happening right now. The wave is already the ocean.

So let us not keep superficiality shallow.

CHAPTER 40

Don't Give Fear a Thought

When fearfulness infects you, don't mind it. Neither avoid it nor let it recruit your mind. Don't give it a thought.

Approach the infected areas with care. No antibiotic heroics, no psychosurgical wizardry, just ordinary everyday caring.

Touch the infection with undivided attention, while letting the raw reality of it touch you, penetrate you, shake you more awake. Make contact, intimate contact, allowing it to breathe, allowing to it vibrate, sound off, even grieve. Stop treating it like an adversary or disease.

When approached with sufficient care, fearfulness helps fuel our entry into a quality of openness wherein we cannot be threatened.

Fearfulness is our personified sense of separateness having a bad day. Being invested in making a self out of our apparent separateness guarantees fearfulness. Nevertheless, the arising of fearfulness, however compelling, does not mean that *we* are afraid, but rather only that fear is present, coexisting with varying degrees of awareness of it.

When fearfulness does manage to infiltrate your mind, read its contents once-through as though they belonged to a supermarket tabloid, taking careful note of which headlines most easily snare your attention. Then *immediately* shift your attention, and shift it completely, to the physical correlates of your fearfulness, resisting the temptation to scoot back into your thinking mind. Tour the somatic nooks, crannies, and grottos of your fearfulness, paying close attention to its textures, tones, directionality, shapings, and other anatomical peculiarities. Note that it is not static, not a noun, not a something inhabiting you, but rather a verb, a process, always on the move, riddled with impermanence.

Then ask yourself exactly WHO or WHAT it is that's feeling fearful. Is it really *you*? Find out. As you discover—and not just intellectually—that the awareness of fear is not itself at all afraid, then you can approach "your" fearfulness with a considerable degree of ease and spaciousness.

When we are sufficiently uprooted to be standing our true ground, we are positioned to be awakened by all things, including fearfulness

The teacher is everywhere. Every moment is a potential crucible for awakening. It's all a setup—set up by all—for realizing, totally realizing, what we actually are, asking only for undreaming eyes.

Fearfulness not only disturbs our sleep, but also can scare us scriptless. At that point—which may last for only a few seconds—we are so divested of our usual dramatics that we are the very openness for which we have yearned. All we have to do is not flee to the surface—like a dreamer desperately trying to exit a nightmare—but remain where we are. Then, into the openness that we are will flood all that is needed.

When we remain outside our fear, we remain trapped within it.

When we, however, consciously get inside our fear, it's as if it turns inside out. Getting inside our fear with wakeful attention and compassion actually expands (or everts) our fear beyond itself. Once the contractedness at the center of fear ceases to be fueled, fear unravels, dissipates, terminates its occupancy of us.

In entering our fear, we end our fear of it.

Through attending closely, caringly, and carefully to the particulars of our fearfulness, we *decentralize* it, so that its intentions and viewpoint can no longer govern us. When the light goes on in the grottos of dread, then fear is little more than Life-energy having a bad day. When we touch our fear with authentic caring, it de-tenses, de-compresses, usually quite quickly becoming something other than fear, something unburdened by fearful agendas or headlines. Fear met with an open heart does not usually take long to dissolve.

The key is to actively and decisively *disidentify* with our fear.

Don't give fearfulness a thought. Instead, give it your full attention. Go to its core. Its dark heart is but the shell, the calcified chambering, of a Love beyond imagination, a Love that effortlessly dissolves all fear.

CHAPTER 41

Second Innocence

Innocence is commonly associated with a childlike lack of knowledge and experience, an infectious guilelessness, an almost deified blamelessness and purity. Behind such formidable cover, the apparently innocent seem to be but powerless pawns, perfect victims, fetchingly haloed photogenic magnets for cultural sentimentality.

As much as innocence is equated with weakness (however endearing) and helplessness (however cute), it is also equated with exploitability. That is, to be innocent is to be very easily manipulated, like infants or young children or "primitive" indigenous cultures. For many, innocence is appealingly naive, adorably or refreshingly unsophisticated. It is abundantly endowed with both prerational openness and ignorance in the Forrest Gumpian nude. And it is unconscious.

But there is a second innocence, a conscious innocence. It is not naive, nor gullible, nor helpless before parental or social tyrannies. It is childlike but not childish. It is open but not defenseless. Its vulnerability is not a liability, but a source of strength. It is not a victim. Its scars both ennoble and deepen it, without reducing its capacity for Wonder. Its sacrifices both root and wing it.

The lack of such innocence militates against real maturity, leaving little more than adulterated stances, make-believe grown-ups, ruined children, aberrated adolescents. When Jesus talked about becoming as little children in order to enter Heaven, he was encouraging neither regression nor naiveté, but rather a conscious innocence. Beginner's mind, lover's heart.

147

Second innocence spontaneously combines the incorruptible openness, the liberating exuberance, the natural playfulness, the sobering joy, and the knowledge-transcending wisdom of unsullied Being. Even the blackest of circumstances cannot obscure its shine. Second innocence shines perhaps most brightly and purely in the faces of great spiritual realizers like Ramana Maharshi, probably the most remarkable Indian sage of the last century. In his unfathomably tender gaze, there is no lack of knowledge or experience, and nor is there any sign of weakness or helplessness. His is boundlessly illuminated innocence, compassionate without trying to be compassionate, overflowing with the innate radiance of Being.

Second innocence is wakeful, everfresh openness, as pure in its silence as in its spontaneity. It is the playground of Being.

We tend to associate innocence with childhood, as if it's something we must outgrow, leave behind, or control (or slip back into caricatures of, as in senility or the excesses of romanticism and sentimentality). So we generally confine innocence to the prepubescent young, tolerating it most of all in babies, even as we, more often than not, proceed to colonize their wilderness of Being with our unresolved wounds. Very young children are also innocent, though usually less so than infants, especially as their seedling egocentricity asserts itself (both as a natural development, and also as a defense mechanism).

Children frequently lose much of their innocence quite early, especially as self-consciousness (which is not actually consciousness, but rather only a painfully critical, shame-rooted viewing of one's apparent self as through the eyes of others) takes root. Those children who become beggars for applause often adopt an adult-pleasing "innocence," exploiting their cuteness and talents, while drifting away from their depths and true innocence. In many of those children who don't lose or don't have to abort their innocence, there often is an exaggerated resistance to letting go of childhood when it's time to do so—and who can blame them, given how much of what awaits them is the soul-barren consumerist frenzy and corresponding depression of ruined childhood and its obsessively adolescent progeny?

An "innocent" adult is generally viewed as a sucker, a fool, a mark, a pushover, an easy target, a primitive, an incompleteness sorely in need of some worldly "education" and some "straightening out" (the extreme of such "awakenings" being that of Euro-American aboriginal genocide). The innocent gaze of an infant is loudly approved of, but such a look from an adult easily creates discomfort in the very same infant-admirers, simply because it invites back a reciprocal openness, an openness that may have been long-denied, fled, or suppressed. Then innocence, especially in its purity, becomes a threat, a too-open stare, an unwanted reminder of what has been lost, crushed, or disowned in one.

With an ease rooted in numbness and emotional illiteracy, we again and again crush, ignore, patronize, tame, mow down, school, or merely romanticize innocence, confusing suppression with care and the loss of Wonder with being grown-up. Nevertheless, the cries of abandoned or aborted innocence haunt even the most hardened of us, as when we nurse a drink in some dark corner, secretly holding our tears at bay. Though the voice of our own innocence may encounter deafness on our part, it is still heard somewhere beneath our skin, if only as the tiniest of fists beating against the inside of our chest.

On some familiar street a heartbroken child suffocating behind an adult mask catches our suddenly sensitized eye—we are busy multi-tasking, caught up in a traffic jam of important elsewheres, but we have to stop. We forget to glance at our watch. Our eyes truly open. The mask quickly becomes transparent, eloquently unraveling and thinning, hauling in our attention like a prodigal kite. Everything is very still, dynamically still. No thought can intrude. No should can trespass here. We cannot look away. Seeing occurs. It is our face, our primal need, our naked innocence. The street disappears. So do we. Breathing continues. And innocence reappears, now become second innocence, weaving through all that we are, like the string of a necklace through its beads.

And through, through the gates we go, without fanfare and fuss, entering Awakening's heartland.

Second innocence.

CHAPTER 42

What Happens After Death?

What happens after death is happening right now.

But what *is* actually happening right now? Not what seems to be happening, but what is, at this very moment, *really* happening?

Death is *now*. Change—and death is but relatively radical change—is now.

Before death, Life. During death, Life. After death, Life.

Life outlives us, until we fully recognize that we are Life itself, and more.

Death does not kill us, but avoiding death deadens us.

We may think that death is the opposite of Life, but the real opposite of death is birth. We are not just birthed into Life, but also die into Life. It's a matter of directionality, depending on which way the door is swinging. It seems that we appear, and then, a lifetime later, disappear, but in reality we are only here, much like the space in a room in which objects arrive, are positioned, and depart.

Imagine a room with no walls or floor or ceiling, no boundaries at all—pure space. And then imagine that this space is sentient. Absolutely sentient. And not only that, but also utterly nonseparate from whatever objects might appear to be appearing in it. It's beyond imagination. That's us.

Us? Yes, beyond all the fuss, and not really even an "us." Nor even a cosmic "I"—just What-Really-Matters in the radical raw. In short, God.

When the lovers wrapped together in ecstatic surrender cry out as one, "Oh God God Oh God!" they are giving accurate voice to what is really going on. The sacred succulence, the sweet dynamite that is turning their flesh into naked energy radiantly alive, is simply Divinity on the loose. In the enormous welcome of such love, God is plugged-in. A ravishing electricity coupled with boundless space.

The more we open, the greater the gift we are given, so long as we don't take it personally. Life is a gift. So is death. There could just as easily be nothing at all. (Some sages have said that there is in fact nothing at all, but we would do well to hear such proclamations with more than our rational minds, for the "nothing" they speak of is not the "nothing" of everyday speech.)

If Life could be said to be the Poetry of Being, then we are the instruments through which that Poetry, that Divine Music, is communicated. Death not only provides the necessary stops, the pauses that refresh, but also permits the evolution of the instruments. Thus is the music enlivened and enriched.

We don't make the music, but without us it cannot be made.

And though this music is immortal, its beauty is forged and evolves through an ongoing intimacy with mortality. Death is the ultimate blacksmith's furnace, dissolving all forms. It is the darkest shade of black and yet is also ablaze with light. Darkness shining wild. Life already blooming with child. Bits of upstart green splitting fields of concrete.

What happens after Death is, as always, already happening now. Your body exhales, pauses, and—mundane magic—in comes another breath, already seeded with its death, yet also filled with undying Life.

Life is, among other things, a near-death experience.

There's so much we're dying to see, dying to be.

Dying to live.

CHAPTER 43

We Are Not "In" a Body

We cannot go out of the body because we are not in a body.

The body is in us.

What *is* within is our physical, mental, and emotional makeup, noted and navigated (mostly unconsciously) by our attention. But just *who* is doing, or is behind, this noting and navigating? No one in particular. As mystical or deep transpersonal experience demonstrates, there is no discrete entity inside, no tenured tenant, no independent inner dweller, but rather only the *personification*—or, more precisely, the personalized *dramatization*—of the movement and focal coalescings of attention through our body and mind. Hearing occurs, awareness of hearing simultaneously occurs, and we typically act as if we are the "hearer," when in fact there is, as the Buddhas have taught, no one inside doing the hearing.

What we essentially are makes its appearance not *in* a body, but *as* a body. This does not necessarily mean that we literally *are* our body, but that our body expresses rather than contains us.

But what about OOBEs (out-of-the-body experiences)? Does not their existence prove that we are *in* a body? Not necessarily. They simply show that substantial dissociation from the physical is possible at times other than when we are sleeping. We don't then so much exit from the body as let the body exit from us; we are then conscious, but not embodied-conscious. The sense of separation that characterizes an OOBE may be simply that, a sense of separation or tangible apartness, perhaps triggered by the settling of attention in zones of the brain that are ordinarily activated through intense shock or stress. Some of those who endured horrendous abuse as children have said they watched the violation of themselves from somewhere close to the ceiling. Pure survival.

Though some OOBEs might possibly occur beyond or even independent of the physical body, the majority of OOBEs may simply be taking place in subtle, or seemingly non-physical, regions of the bodymind, registering their presence through the very same mechanisms as "ordinary" experience. Many OOBEs may also be lucid dreams (dreams in which one knows that one is dreaming) that are only partially lucid and therefore are taken literally, as though one, for example, is indeed standing a few feet away from one's sleeping body, rather than simply dreaming that one is doing so.

According to various wisdom-traditions, at death the body is shed, dropped, let go of, but we, or something resembling us, persists. The physical dimension of the body drops off—or is radically deconstructed—at death, and we, so the transpersonal story usually goes, ordinarily feel lighter and freer for a while, as if bodiless, but before very long typically assume another bodymind, perhaps more rarefied than our earth-bodymind, but nonetheless as seemingly real as the body we had in our just-departed life was to us.

And so we apparently move—or are irresistibly moved—through dreamlike realms pulsating with the fleshed-out consequences of our life's dominant habits and hungers, as well as with the possibility of a truer life. Sooner or later, the story continues, those longings of ours that are less than our longing for full awakening inexorably draw us toward another round of waking-state physical embodiment—unless there is full recognition that all that is occurring is but dreamplay—thereby mechanically fulfilling the current blueprint encoded throughout "us" both by our needs and by what we are *doing* with those needs.

But we don't have to die to experience this process. It's happening right now, even as we dream that we aren't dreaming.

We are what we are seeking, but our attention is usually elsewhere, enslaved to the mindset that makes a goal out of what is *already* the case. We'll look anywhere but inside our looking. How can we find What-Really-Matters, when we never truly lost It? Call it God's Joke. What's uncorked by getting the joke is the realization that we have been doing, among other things, some very serious dreaming, pretending we *are* the roles we play in our dreams, especially the role that features "our" body.

The key is to witness—and, as much as possible, unguardedly feel—our body with unmuddied attention, not from a mentalized or compartmentalized distance, nor from a supposedly higher or ascended consciousness (which makes just more distance, however spiritually correct it may seem), but *directly*, letting awareness and sensation meet with minimal mediation or buffering or sedation.

A rare subtlety is called for here, along with a willingness to microscopically explore the edge of the edge. Perceive your body from a place of no-distance. This, done deeply and without rehearsal, helps us to navigate toward the very heart of primordial vitality and openness.

To thus feel our body, to sense its multileveled energetics and deep structures with such care, is an art in which compassion, patience, and the spirit of exploration all coexist. In the map-eluding Wonderland that the body "becomes" when we thus feel it, we meet God in the flesh, God-as-flesh. Then our physicality, in intimate embrace with wide-open yet still finely-tuned awareness, becomes an embodiment of the Source of the body. God incarnate.

This is simultaneously no big deal and mind-blowingly real. Eventually, we feel-intuit God not only with little amoebic extensions of ourselves, but with our *entirety*. Such feeling-intuiting is not a matter of being inside or outside our physicality, but rather is about letting our whole being, even in its densest or most seemingly solid dimensions, resonate and dance with God. The ultimate participatory act.

The body asks only to be loved, lived, and illuminated. The body is not some separate mass, but is continuous—and not just elementally—

with all that is. The body is but precipitated Being, Light incarnate, prismed into form. It is not just matter. (And for that matter, matter is not just matter.) The body is not a burden with which we've been saddled. It is not an obstruction to realizing God.

We need to shift from having a body to *being* a body, and from being a body to *Being*. Even when the body dissolves in ecstasy or deep peace, it still exists as God's Body, pregnant with form.

In permitting a fuller, saner embodiment of our essential nature, we make possible a life for ourselves that is of benefit to all, regardless of our moods and circumstances, regardless of the dramatics of purification. In this, we develop a radical intimacy both with what dies and with what does not die.

Embodiment arises, unexplainably and with hyperbole-shattering import and beauty, seeded with an evolutionary imperative that makes possible the eventual emergence of self-organizing and ultimately self-conscious structures through which suffering's myriad classrooms can become places of healing and Homecoming.

All the worlds are here in this very moment, dreamily coexisting, their common key floating in the heart of incarnation's flesh-dance. Know your body without using your intellect, except perhaps as an aide in initial scouting scans. Allow intrinsic awareness to tour and explore your body until it is obvious that your body is not yours, but is simply Energy, Consciousness on the move, elementally and feelingly and paradoxically continuous with all that is.

It is crucial that we not only love what outlives this body, but this body also, for it too is a weaving of the Real, a unique flowering whose rise and beauty and singularity ache to be known before its demise.

This piece has no end. Nor does the body.

CHAPTER 44

Who Has Room for Emptiness?

Who has space for Emptiness? Who has time for Eternity? Who among the lonely has room for Solitude? Whatever it is that drives us out of the traffic jam behind our forehead invites us into nothing but Light.

The Universe is pure fontanelle. The lid was never really on.

Awareness makes an appearance, showing up in and as something novel, dressed for the occasion. Infinite appearances.

Gravity and Light continue to come together, birthing all, consuming all, being all. To the Consciousness that is the subjective dimension of Light, Gravity is but Primal attraction, Love in the absolute raw.

As Emptiness—the *Mahashunyata*, or primordial Reality, of Buddhism—is made into a "nondualistic" goal and metaphysical conversation-stopper, Time lines us up, neatly sectioning our sky, leaving us as special nobodies. Spiritual ambition does not die easily. So easy to make not being special something special. Look around, look inside your looking, look without looking, letting the ashes of this and other Zenigmatic sentences dangle like smudged sighs somewhere high above your neocortical scurrying and worrying, slowly confettiing down upon the intruders stationed in your head.

How does it feel to be food for thought?

We keep trying to think our way out, reducing ourselves to lottery stubs in the Great Getaway's spinning barrel. Thus does Truth get obscured by well-schooled facts. Amnesia sends Christmas cards to itself. Understanding chokes on its own tracks. Is Earth but a cosmic reform school? Vagrant phrases keep breaking in. Explanations only affirm the Mystery. And we raggedly limp around our quarantined pain in poisoned playgrounds, confusing numbness and detachment, faith and hope, vacuity and openness, anger and aggression, guilt and conscience, suffering and pain, wisdom and knowledge, madness and sanity.

Emptiness appears to recognize the gravity of the situation, trapping enough light to make something of Itself. All sorts of somethings, somewhens, somebodies, a few taking shape as astrophysicists dallying like voyeuristic sperm around the perimeter of Black Holes, staying just far enough away so as to not get sucked in, swallowed, consumed, emptied. Few are those men who can give themselves fully to a woman without eviscerating themselves. Virility and vulnerability reach for each other in broken rooms, trailing clouds of war. All the boys bleeding to death or locked away in their headquarters, while the sky burns like a screaming steak and the forests fall without a sound.

There are no winners in this overtime. Is designing umbrellas for acid rain really progress? Spiritual seekers with polyester smiles and orphaned shadows sit in the twilight, constipated with hope. Cynics wait for them to crash and burn. Others open the windows, letting the night rush in, blazing with light. Darkness shining wild.

The Storm is already here. The empires have fallen apart. Chaos is seeking annulment of its marriage to Order, claiming mental cruelty. World leaders' memoirs are on sale, crayons sold separately. We sneer, but do not go to the heart of our fear, hiding out in our slumber and greed, ashamed of our real need.

Nevertheless, Silence never ceased. Nor did Love. Emptiness never ceased. The Wilderness of Being, the Wonder that cannot be imagined. Words come slowly now, like lead-dipped feathers, dissolving in formless yet overwhelmingly tangible Presence, this page now a sea of fast-darkening white, this breath not mine, this gap between you and me but an entrancing fiction into which we read meaning before it all shatters.

Only Emptiness has room for all, only Love can touch all, only Silence can express all.

Stretching for one more sentence, I watch my speechless words aflame in the Holy Wild, leaving no ashes, but only gratitude.

About the Author

Since 1978 Robert has worked as a psychotherapist, group leader, and teacher of spiritual deepening practices, integrating the physical, mental, emotional, and spiritual in his work. He holds a Ph.D. in Psychology and has worked worldwide. Robert is known not only for the depth, creativity, and transformative power of his sessions and groupwork, but also for his critically acclaimed books (including *The Way of the Lover* and *Love Must Also Weep*) and essays (which have appeared in publications ranging from *Magical Blend* to the *Journal of Transpersonal Psychology*, as well as in several anthologies). He lives in Crescent Beach, British Columbia.

For more on his work and writing, visit **www.robertmasters.com**.

ISBN 141203633-X